The Delight

Gluten-Free

C O O K B O O K

The Delight Gluten-Free

COOKBOOK

Vanessa Maltin Weisbrod

Executive Editor of *Delight Gluten-Free Magazine*

Photography by Janice Cuevas, Jennifer Dunlap, Gabrielle Hoffman,
Julie Luse and Vanessa Maltin Weisbrod

The Delight Gluten-Free Cookbook

ISBN-13: 978-0-373-89305-8

Library of Congress Cataloging-in-Publication Data

Weisbrod, Vanessa Maltin.

The delight gluten-free cookbook : 150 delicious recipes / Vanessa Maltin Weisbrod, executive editor of Delight Gluten-Free Magazine ;
photography by Janice Cuevas, Jennifer Dunlap, Gabrielle Hoffman, Julie Luse and Vanessa Maltin Weisbrod.

pages cm

Includes index.

ISBN 978-0-373-89305-8 (alk. paper)

1. Gluten-free diet--Recipes. I. Title.

RM237.86.W45 2014

641.3--dc23

2014005170

www.Harlequin.com

Printed in U.S.A.

To everyone living a gluten-free lifestyle.
May every meal you eat be full of
flavor, love and spice.

Contents

✪ = Fan Favorite

3 Soups & Salads   78

4 Snacks   94

5 Vegetables & Side Dishes 120

✪ = Fan Favorite

6 Main Dishes 148

7 Desserts 182

8 Cocktails   234

Converting to Metrics   248

Index   249

About the Author   257

✪ = Fan Favorite

Acknowledgments and Our Foodie Staff

The heart of *Delight Gluten-Free Magazine* is our staff. We are professional foodies who want to eat, cook and enjoy delicious food in our homes, out on the town and around the world. We just happen to be on gluten-free diets. Every single day we go to work with the goal of bringing our readers a gluten-free world filled with delightful options, one flavor-packed meal at a time.

So how do we do it?

We eat constantly. To create recipes, one must understand the origin of flavors and textures. Whether it's traditional American fare or foods from around the world, it's imperative that we appreciate what goes into the food we cook.

There's one rule in our office: Taste everything (unless a food will make you ill, of course). We taste spices, sauces, flours, grains, chocolates, herbs, jams, coffees, liqueurs . . . you name it and it's probably touched our taste buds this year! We sit around our conference table discussing how ingredients taste, how they affect our palates and how we can incorporate them into recipes. Then we go into our test kitchen and start experimenting.

This book would not have been possible without an amazing team, all working together. Whether it was developing recipes, spending hundreds of hours in the kitchen testing recipes at least three times each, orchestrating photo shoots, calculating nutritional data, browsing grocery store shelves for new products or copy editing, everyone played a huge role in putting together the content of this book. Thank you to each of the following individuals for dedicating so much time to making this book so beautiful and tasty: Sally Pickle, Janice Cuevas, Jordan Gary, Torie Foster, Jennifer Dunlap, Gabrielle Hoffman, Emily Freedner, Tiffany Janes, Jennifer Stearns and our wonderful interns, Sara Benner and Kristin Grant.

Special thanks to my enthusiastic, energetic and inspiring agent Maura Teitlebaum, who is so generous with her guidance and support. I am so lucky to have you as part of my team. And finally, to my wonderful editors at Harlequin—Sarah Pelz and Rebecca Hunt. I am truly appreciative of your constant enthusiasm for this book and your dedication to inspiring the gluten-free community to cook delicious food.

Introduction

Why start a gluten-free magazine? The answer is simple. Everyone—regardless of a food allergy or intolerance—should eat incredible food every single day. It should look beautiful and taste like heaven. But, most important, the recipes should work every single time in the same way for experienced chefs and home cooks alike.

If you sit down with people who love food and are also diagnosed with celiac disease or have a sensitivity to gluten, you'll often hear the same story. Before their diagnosis, they eagerly awaited the arrival of their favorite food magazines every month and as soon as they appeared, they read them cover to cover, tearing out the most beautiful images of carefully crafted meals. They ate with their eyes first, picking recipes with photographs that made their mouths water. They planned family meals, holiday gatherings and social events around the flavors on the pages. A food magazine was their kitchen bible, offering new ideas and fresh flavors every thirty days.

And then they couldn't eat gluten. In an instant, more than 90 percent of the recipes in their favorite food magazines were no longer suitable for their special diet. They could take a risk by experimenting with substitutes, but oftentimes that only resulted in failed attempts and lost ingredients. So they let their subscriptions lapse and fell into a pattern of boring meals and uninspired cooking.

Delight Gluten-Free Magazine launched in 2008 with one simple mission: to inspire, educate and encourage food lovers to embrace a gluten-free lifestyle filled with bold flavors, fresh ingredients and beautiful food. We believe that you don't have to—in fact, you shouldn't—feel deprived if you follow a gluten-free diet, and this belief is at the heart of every issue and recipe we publish.

From day one, the magazine was a gathering of people who loved food and had a shared vision of creating a sinfully satisfying gluten-free experience for readers. The first issue (Winter 2008) shipped to approximately 3,000 people. It was complimentary, so we hoped that readers would love the recipes (which included crusty popovers, butternut squash risotto, French toast, duck breast with chocolate and coffee sauce, chocolate truffle cake, mini pavlovas and tiramisu, among many others), and then subscribe. They did.

Five years later, *Delight* became the global leader of gluten-free and food allergy publications with the best and most relevant content. We are a team of food professionals offering seasonal, inspired and well-tested recipes to our readers. Today, the magazine has print readers across North America (United States, Canada and Mexico), as well as in Spain, Singapore, Greece, Thailand, Hong Kong, Belgium, Germany, Israel, New Zealand, Australia and the United Kingdom. Consumers can also read each issue of the digital edition of the magazine on an Apple or Android device. And more than half a million users visit the *Delight Gluten-Free Magazine* website every month to indulge in recipes, travel guides and in-depth articles.

I sincerely hope that this cookbook will become the go-to resource for your gluten-free cooking needs. For newly diagnosed readers, this will be a tool for adjusting to the gluten-free lifestyle—setting up a gluten-free kitchen, purchasing the right products and adjusting recipes to fit a gluten-free mold. For experienced gluten-free foodies, it's a tribute to how delicious food can be with innovative recipes, adventures in gluten-free baking and inspired food and cocktail pairings. In addition to the 125 original recipes, you'll also indulge in some of *Delight*'s all-time fan favorite recipes! It's exactly what our *Delight* family always envisioned: *gluten-free food filled with flavor, love and spice.*

Vanessa Maltin Weisbrod
Delight *Executive Editor*

CHAPTER ONE

Gluten-Free Made Easy

1

The Gluten-Free Diet and Food Labeling

A gluten-free lifestyle can be tasty, nutritious and full of flavor—you just have to do it right. With a solid understanding of gluten-free ingredients and how to properly use them, you'll have no trouble creating mouthwatering meals for your family. Ahead you'll learn all about safe gluten-free ingredients, navigating your local grocery store, selecting products and tips for keeping your family healthy. Let's get started!

Why Start a Gluten-Free Diet?

There are many reasons to start a gluten-free diet. Most people venture into the world of gluten-free eating because they have been diagnosed with celiac disease (an autoimmune condition), a gluten sensitivity or a wheat allergy. The only current treatment for these conditions is a 100 percent lifelong gluten-free diet. No cheating, no tasting. You've got to be gluten-free all the time.

Others have started a gluten-free diet to improve their daily nutritional intake and others to lose weight. While heated controversy surrounds the use of a gluten-free diet for weight loss, we can all agree that living a naturally gluten-free lifestyle rich in fruits, vegetables, protein and whole gluten-free grains, can be a nutritious and fulfilling way to structure a low-calorie diet.

Whatever their reasoning may be, with millions of individuals around the world adopting a gluten-free diet, the marketplace has responded with exponential growth in the development of high-quality gluten-free products.

Today, gluten-free foods have their own sections in grocery stores, and restaurants choose to highlight gluten-free dishes on their menus. Previously unheard-of grains, flours, seeds and nuts, like quinoa, teff, amaranth, chia, almond meal and coconut flour have become household staples and main ingredients in recipes for cookies, cakes, pizza crusts, muffins and more. Manufacturers have changed their packaging to boast bold gluten-free symbols and some have even altered ingredients in popular products to capture the gluten-free market. It's now all about the highest-quality, best-tasting food for this vibrantly expanding community.

What Is Gluten?

Gluten is a protein found in all forms of wheat, rye and barley. It is most commonly found in food, but it also hides in medicine, vitamins and makeup. The first thing you should do when starting a gluten-free diet is schedule a meeting with a skilled dietitian or nutritionist. A well-trained professional can help you learn the basics of a gluten-free diet and help you find ways to adapt to your new lifestyle.

When you're at home or at the grocery store, a quick guide to ingredients can be a helpful tool for determining if a packaged product is safe. Below is *Delight*'s quick guide to identifying safe and unsafe ingredients.

Safe Gluten-Free Ingredients

Eliminating wheat, barley and rye from your diet may seem like a daunting task, but it's important to remember that there are still hundreds of grains and other foods that you can eat. Staples like fresh fruits and vegetables, meats, poultry, seafood and most types of dairy are all gluten-free in their natural forms.

Acorn Flour	Coconut Flour	Hominy	Sesame
Almond Flour	Corn	Instant Rice	Sorghum
Amaranth	Corn Flour	Kasha	Soy
Arborio Rice	Corn Gluten	Lentils	Soybeans
Arrowroot	Corn Meal	Millet	Sunflower Seeds
Baker's Yeast	Cornstarch	Modified Cornstarch	Sweet Rice Flour
Basmati Rice	Cottonseed	Modified Tapioca	Tapioca
Bean Flours	Dal	Montina	Tapioca Flour
Brown Rice	Dasheen Flour	Peanut Flour	Taro Flour
Brown Rice Flour	Enriched Rice	Potato Flour	Teff
Buckwheat	Fava Bean	Potato Starch	Tofu
Calrose Rice	Flax	Quinoa	White Rice Flour
Canola	Flax Seeds	Red Rice	Xanthan Gum
Cassava	Garbanzo	Rice Bran	Yeast
Chana	Glutinous Rice	Rice Flour	Yucca
Chestnut	Gram Flour	Risotto	
Chickpea Flour	Guar Gum	Sago	

Safe Food Additives

When purchasing packaged foods, there will likely be many ingredients listed that sound unfamiliar. Below is a list of food additives that are safe for a gluten-free diet.

Acacia Gum	Celluose	Maltodextrin	Stearic Acid
Adipic Acid	Corn Syrup	Maltol	Sucralose
Algin	Cream of Tartar	Mannitol	Sucrose
Annatto	Dextrose	Methylcellulose	Sugar
Aspartame	Distilled Vinegar	Monosodium Glutamate	Tartaric Acid
Baking Yeast	Ethyl Maltol	Papain	Tartrazine
Benzoic Acid	Fructose	Pectin	Titanium Dioxide
Beta Carotene	Fumaric Acid	Polysorbate	Vanilla Bean
BHA	Gelatin	Propylene Glycol	Vanilla Extract
BHT	Glucose	Psyllium	Xylitol
Brown Sugar	Invert Sugar	Sodium Benzonate	Yam
Calcium Disodium	Karaya Gum	Sodium Metabisulphite	Yeast; Autolyzed
Carrageenan	Lactic Acid	Sodium Nitrate	Autolyzed Yeast Extract
Caramel Coloring	Lactose	Sodium Sulphite	Nutritional Yeast
Carboxymethyl	Lecithin	Sorbitol	
Carob Bean Gum	Malic Acid	Spices (100% pure)	

Unsafe Foods

Below is a list of basic food items that contain gluten. When purchasing prepared foods, always be on the lookout for these key words. It's important to note that this is not a complete list of gluten-containing foods. If you're ever unsure about the safety of a product, call the manufacturer directly.

Barley	Couscous	Kamut	Rye
Barley Enzymes	Dextrin	Macha	Seitan
Barley Extract	Durum	Malt	Spelt
Barley Grass	Einkorn	Malt Flavoring	Semolina
Barley Malt	Emmer	Malt Syrup	Sprouted Wheat
Barley Pearls	Farina	Malt Vinegar	Tabbouleh
Bran	Fu	Matzo	Triticale
Bleached Flour	Graham	Mir	Wheat
Bulgur	Hordeum Vulgare	Rice Malt	Wheat Starch
Bulgur Wheat	Hydrolyzed Wheat Protein	Rice Syrup	

Food Labeling Laws in the United States

In August 2013, the Food and Drug Administration (FDA) issued a final rule in the United States that defines what characteristics a food must have in order to be labeled as "gluten-free." The rule also holds foods labeled "without gluten," "free of gluten" and "no gluten" to the same standard.

The FDA set the standard for food products labeled as gluten-free to contain less than 20 parts per million (ppm), a level that has repeatedly been endorsed by leading celiac disease experts, including Dr. Alessio Fasano of the Center for Celiac Research at Massachusetts General Hospital for Children. The 20-ppm level is the lowest level that can consistently be detected in food using currently available scientific analytical tools. The standard is also consistent with similar laws in other countries and international bodies that determine food safety standards.

What does this mean? When looking at food labels at the grocery store, if the product boasts the claim of being gluten-free in the United States, you'll know that it must contain less than 20 ppm of gluten as specified by the FDA.

Navigating the Grocery Store for At-Home Cooking

The day you're diagnosed with celiac disease or a sensitivity to gluten, everything changes about the way you'll shop for groceries. While a trip to the supermarket used to be a breeze, it now feels like the same local grocery store is a place you barely recognize. It's very easy to become overwhelmed, but all of us at *Delight* encourage you to take a deep breath and try to see all the great possibilities that still exist within the same store. With just a little extra patience and an open mind, your grocery store will soon become a flavorful portal to your continued health and wellness. And breezing through each aisle will become second nature again in no time!

Shopping the Perimeter

It's best to get to know your grocery store's perimeter, or what we like to refer to as the "safety zone." It's the best place for the gluten-free consumer to start shopping because that's where most stores keep their natural, unprocessed foods, like produce, dairy and meat.

Fruits, Vegetables and Dairy

All fresh fruits and vegetables are naturally gluten-free. These whole foods pack a nutritious punch, and you can create endless meals from this section alone. Dairy is also naturally gluten-free, which means that milk, yogurt, cheese, sour cream and butter are all options for you. Just be cautious with any items that are flavored or include other foods you can mix in, like yogurt with granola. The good news is that over the last several years, companies have started putting bold gluten-free labels on most dairy products that are safe, so be on the lookout for a gluten-free callout.

Meat, Poultry and Seafood

Meat, poultry and seafood are also completely gluten-free in their natural state. Items like chicken breasts, baby back ribs, salmon, steaks, pork chops, shrimp and eggs are all on the menu. You can boost the flavor of these protein sources with spices and gluten-free marinades and by cooking them on the stove, in the oven or on the grill. Yum!

Also on store shelves in the meat section are a variety of flavored sausages packed with tangy combinations of unique ingredients, like chicken, mango, apples, cheeses and herbs. The majority of these items are naturally gluten-free (and the packages say so boldly), but again, always double-check the label to be extra cautious. Note that some deli meats and marinated foods may not be gluten-free, so always check the labels.

Frozen Foods Aisle

The most basic items you'll come across in this section are frozen fruits, vegetables, meats and fish. Remember: All fruits, vegetables and unprocessed meats are naturally gluten-free. Just make sure they haven't been packaged with any gluten-containing flavor packets, seasonings, breading or sauces.

If you ever don't have time to make one of the delicious recipes in this book, the frozen food aisle offers plenty of gluten-free ready-to-heat meals and frozen baked goods that come in handy in a pinch.

Baking Aisle

At first diagnosis, most people immediately direct their sorrow toward baked goods. It's hard to accept that some of your favorite treats may not be gluten-free. But please don't be discouraged because there are just so many options available! No craving will go unsatisfied! (Turn to Chapters 2, 4 and 7 for some new favorites to try.)

A word of caution about oats and oat flour: in their natural form, oats are gluten-free, but it is difficult for companies in the United States to guarantee that oats aren't contaminated while processing, storing or transporting. Look for companies that sell safe, gluten-free oats and oat flour that are processed in dedicated factories, and discuss oat consumption with your dietitian.

Gluten-Free Flour

There are a variety of substitutions for traditional wheat flour, like brown and white rice, sorghum, chickpea, corn, millet, teff, buckwheat, quinoa, soybean, oat, coconut and almond flour. There are also many safe starches, including cornstarch, potato starch and tapioca starch. Many gluten-free brands offer these items. You can substitute them in recipes and create delightful gluten-free alternatives to your favorite baked goods.

You may also need to supplement your recipes with xanthan gum or guar gum, which act as a "glue" in gluten-free baking. These might be in the health food section of your grocery store if they're not in the baking aisle. Many companies also offer gluten-free all-purpose flours, if you're looking for something that's pre-mixed. Check out our guide on pages 14–15 to choosing the right gluten-free all-purpose flour or recipes for making your own blend at home.

Baking Mixes

If convenience is what you're looking for, keep an eye out for the many gluten-free baking mixes available. They offer everything from cookies, cakes, pie crusts and pancakes to bread, muffins and pizza dough. Even major companies like Betty Crocker, Bisquick and King Arthur Flour offer these mixes, but they're not the only ones, so have fun exploring!

Luckily, many other staples of baking, like sugar, baking powder, baking soda and yeast, are all naturally gluten-free. You may have to do a bit of pre-store research and experimentation, but you'll be making all your favorite recipes in no time!

Keep in mind though, many gluten-free mixes are placed next to gluten-containing ones, so be careful not to pick up the wrong one.

Sauces, Dressings and Condiments

It's not often you'll sit down to a dish of dry meat and bare veggies. Often, the centerpiece of a dish is the sauce, dressing or condiments that pull it all together. Some stores have entire aisles dedicated to these items, and plenty of them are gluten-free.

Classic Condiments

Many condiments that are staples in most households—ketchup, mayo, mustard and relish—are very easy to find gluten-free. Heinz has a wide variety of gluten-free ketchup, mustard, mayo and relish. The company's website also has an extensive list of its gluten-free products, which can be helpful to glance over before you head to the store. French's mustards are another good choice.

Pasta Sauce and Salad Dressing

Gluten-free pasta sauce is another item that is very easy to come by. Several mainstream brands offer a wide variety of flavors beyond your typical marinara sauce. As for salad dressing, it feels like there's nearly half an aisle of nothing but salad dressing. That's a lot of labels to read! Before long, you'll have a quick list of favorites, but to get you started, Newman's Own and Hidden Valley definitely offer gluten-free options. Kraft is also very good at labeling its dressings if they contain wheat, barley or rye, so an unsafe product is easy to spot.

Oils and Vinegar

If you prefer to make your own dressings and sauces at home, you'll no doubt be using a variety of oils and vinegars. Luckily, almost all oil is gluten-free, including olive oil, canola oil, coconut oil and vegetable oil, to name a few. If you're buying flavored or seasoned oil, that's when you have to double-check the ingredients. There are also plenty of vinegars that are gluten-free, such as balsamic, apple cider vinegar, rice vinegar and white and red wine vinegar. Malt vinegar, however, is not safe for the gluten-free diet, so steer clear of that vinegar.

Other Flavors

Asian-style sauces are probably where you have to be most careful. Many of them contain wheat, including soy sauce. However, there are several brands that now offer full lines of gluten-free Asian sauces, including soy sauce, fish sauce, curry sauce and teriyaki sauce.

Soy sauce is probably the most common sauce associated with Asian cooking. Traditional soy sauce does contain wheat and, by default, so does any other sauce that uses soy sauce as an ingredient. Fortunately, gluten-free tamari is widely available. San-J is a go-to brand that sells large bottles for your cupboard as well as travel packets that you can slip into your pocket for meals out. The company offers a regular and a light soy sauce. San-J also sells a variety of delicious gluten-free Asian cooking sauces, like Szechuan, teriyaki, sweet and tangy and Asian BBQ. Kikkoman now offers a gluten-free soy sauce as well.

There are also many brands of hot sauce, salsa and barbecue sauces on the grocery store shelves. You'll have to be vigilant about reading the labels if you want to try something fancy or new, but there's a plethora of gluten-free staples in every store.

This section of the store is probably where there will be the greatest mix of gluten-free and gluten-containing products commingling on the shelves. Unless your store has a dedicated gluten-free section, you'll have to be diligent about checking labels until you find your favorite brands and flavors. Many sauces and dressings can easily have more than twenty ingredients on the label. If you're feeling overwhelmed or there are some ingredients you can't even pronounce, find a safer alternative until you've had an opportunity to do a little more research.

Canned Goods Aisle

In an ideal world, we'd cook everything from scratch, using only the freshest ingredients. We'd stew tomatoes and bottle our own sauces, keep the bones from our roast chickens to boil down into broth and maybe even pass gluten-free dough through our pasta makers. But let's be realistic—we're busy! There will be days when hours spent in the kitchen offer a welcome retreat, but sometimes we need to be able to rummage through the pantry and whip something up in a hurry.

Since the invention of canning, pulling off an unplanned meal has become infinitely easier and, fortunately, the convenience is not lost on us gluten-free diners. There are many gluten-free options straight from the can, so grab your openers and head over to the canned goods aisle to check them out!

Beans

Incorporating naturally gluten-free beans into your meals is a great way to boost your fiber and protein intake and can make any dish heartier and more filling.

Black beans are a great addition to any Mexican-style dish, and cannellini beans are perfect for Italian dishes. Kidney beans add bulk to soups and chilies, and chickpeas are an essential source of protein in salads. These are just four popular beans, but there are so many different types of beans to try. Also, you'll be able to choose between regular, low-sodium and no-salt-added varieties.

Fruit and Vegetables

While eating fresh fruits and vegetables is always the more nutritious option, there are times when having the canned variety on hand is great. The shelf life is obviously much longer and can make for a quick source of ingredients. Canned items can also prevent waste when you just need a small amount of something for a recipe, like pineapple to toss into a stir-fry or a handful of artichokes to add to a pasta dish. Canned fruit is also a great option if you're craving something out of season. It also can make for a simple dessert on its own or it can be part of an easy homemade parfait when mixed with yogurt and gluten-free granola. Try to choose a canned fruit that is packed in juice rather than syrup. This will cut down on your sugar intake.

When shopping for canned goods, there are a few things to watch out for. "Heat-and-serve" canned items, like soups and chilies, commonly contain gluten, as do many varieties of baked beans and flavored seafood. Until you find the brands and flavors you have confirmed are gluten-free, remember to be diligent and always check the label!

Setting Up a Gluten-Free Kitchen

Making Food Taste Good: A *Delight* Test Kitchen Tour

The *Delight Gluten-Free Magazine* test kitchen looks just like a home kitchen. We use residential-grade appliances and equipment purchased at traditional kitchen supply stores. Our goal is to test every recipe using equipment that every home cook would have on hand. The only major difference is that we typically celebrate the winter holidays in July and enjoy summer BBQs in the dead of winter! No, we're not totally crazy; we just work that far ahead to create our menus. It's really not that big of a deal until we try to find ripe ruby red watermelons when it's snowing outside!

Here are some of our favorite test kitchen tools, which we think everyone should have at home.

★ **Stand Mixer:** There is no better kitchen tool than a stand mixer. It works as a mixer for batters, a whisk for whipping eggs and cream, and a kneader for dough. With additional attachments, the device also works as a pasta cutter, ice cream machine and meat grinder. While some cooks see the device as a pain to clean, we see it as a kitchen savior. It cuts your prep time in half and saves your arm from hours of whisking, kneading and stirring!

- ★ **Food Processor:** We consider our food processor a blessing with a blade. This machine quickly chops nuts from whole pieces to a soft powder or quickly pulses cold butter into flour to make a perfect pie crust dough. Making mayonnaise? Just drizzle the oil into the eggs while running the food processor and, in seconds, you've made homemade mayo.

- ★ **Immersion Blender:** Trying to purée a soup or gravy in a standing blender is screaming for danger. You run the risk of burning yourself on the pot or in the steam, as well as having an unevenly blended soup or gravy. This handheld tool lets you purée your hot soups right in the original pot. Just place the immersion blender into the pot and blend away. Be careful not to let the blade skim the top of the liquid, however, or you may get sprayed by your supper.

- ★ **Kitchen Torch:** Browning the tops of meringue pies or crème brûlée never works just perfectly under a broiler. Unless you're watching every second, there are inevitably spots that brown more quickly than others. Use a handheld kitchen torch to evenly brown your desserts with ease and complete control. Just be sure to carefully read all of the instructions for the torch you buy to prevent any kitchen fire nightmares.

- ★ **Glass and Metal Baking Dishes:** Choosing the right cookware is one of the most crucial elements for creating a successful recipe. For sweet baked goods like cookies, brownies, muffins and cakes, you'll typically choose a metal baking pan, while savory dishes like casseroles typically cook best in glass baking dishes. Take careful note in each recipe of the type of cookware suggested for use. It's not just a suggestion, but an important step in the recipe.

Preventing Cross-Contamination in Your Kitchen

When you're on a gluten-free diet, staying safe means avoiding any potential sources of cross-contamination. This can happen very easily and unintentionally, so it's important to understand the many ways in which cross-contamination can occur in your own home. While a household does not need to be entirely gluten-free in order to be safe, there are several measures you and your family can take to ensure that boiling water, condiments, frying oil, utensils and food preparation surfaces are sterilized to be safely gluten-free. It's not any more difficult than guarding against bacteria . . . just remember to keep all your kitchen elements clean!

★ **Boiling Water:** If you're making pasta for dinner and decide to make both gluten-free pasta and gluten-containing pasta, the pastas cannot be cooked in the same water. Gluten from the gluten-containing pasta will contaminate the water and make you sick. The same applies to cooking gluten-free items, such as quinoa, rice, vegetables or potatoes in boiling water that has already come in contact with gluten-containing ingredients. Additionally, if the food you're preparing requires straining, be sure that gluten-containing foods go into one strainer while gluten-free items are strained in a separate colander or are strained first.

★ **Condiments:** Any condiment that requires you to dip into it should not be used on both gluten-free and gluten-containing ingredients. Particles from gluten-containing ingredients easily contaminate jars of peanut butter, cream cheese, butter, etc. To be extra cautious, if you live in a mixed gluten household, consider buying separate condiments and label one set as gluten-free. Those eating gluten-free foods should only touch the gluten-free set of condiments. If you don't want to buy doubles of items, have a conversation with your family and/or housemates about scooping out a portion of the item onto a plate before spreading it onto the gluten-containing item so they only dip one time with a clean knife into the container. For other condiments, like ketchup, mustard, mayonnaise and relish, consider buying squeeze bottles to prevent cross-contamination from dipping into the jars.

★ **Cutting Boards:** If you plan to thoroughly scrub a cutting board before and after each use (and you always should), it is completely safe to share with gluten-free and gluten-containing items—assuming you're not using them at the same time. However, if you're worried about cross-contamination, it often helps to have two sets of cutting boards in the kitchen. Consider picking a different-color cutting board for the gluten-free set, so your family can easily identify which board is safe to use. It is also most safe to use plastic or glass cutting boards whenever possible. These boards do not absorb any foods put on them and prevent gluten from sticking to their surface even after washing.

★ **Frying:** Never fry gluten-free and gluten-containing items in the same oil. Particles from the gluten-containing items will inevitably fall into the oil and contaminate the gluten-free foods. Even if you think the oil looks clean, don't trust it. Always use clean oil for your gluten-free foods.

★ **Pots and Pans:** Always wash your pots and pans thoroughly between each use. As long as you're doing a good job washing them, it is safe to cook both gluten-free and gluten-containing items in the same pots and pans. Think of it this way: If you wash your pots and pans well enough to prevent food-borne bacteria from spreading, then you're also cleaning them sufficiently to prevent gluten contamination.

★ **Shelves and Drawers:** Consider designating space within your kitchen storage areas exclusively for gluten-free foods. This will help to visually separate the items that need to be kept free of cross-contamination. If you need to keep gluten-free and gluten-containing items on the same shelves and in the same drawers, always store the gluten-free products above the gluten-containing items. This method will prevent gluten particles from falling into the gluten-free products.

★ **Toasting:** Crumbs quickly accumulate in every single toaster on Earth. There's no way to prevent that from happening. Bread crumbles and creates a massive problem of cross-contamination. If you're willing to wash your toaster in between each use, there is no reason to have separate toasters. However, if you're unable to easily clean out the toaster, or if you feel that your housemates may not be able to keep up with the demand, it may be helpful to have a designated gluten-free toaster. If you use a toaster oven–type device in your home, another option is to always line the racks with foil when toasting gluten-free items. This will prevent cross-contamination and limit the necessity for in-between-use washing. Just be sure to always use clean foil with each use.

★ **Metal or Plastic Utensils:** As with each and every other piece of kitchen equipment, you cannot use the same metal or plastic utensils with gluten-free and gluten-containing items. So, don't go stirring gluten-free gravy with the same spoon that you just used to stir cream of wheat . . . unless you thoroughly washed it in between! Either make the decision to always wash the utensils in between use or purchase a second set of designated gluten-free kitchen equipment.

★ **Wooden Boards, Bowls and Utensils:** Never use wooden kitchen equipment with both gluten-free and gluten-containing foods. Gluten can stick in between the wood grains and even a thorough washing can't get rid of it. Either purchase two sets or avoid wooden equipment altogether if you live in a shared kitchen space.

Gluten-Free All-Purpose Flour Guide

Not all gluten-free flours are created equal. Some are high in starchy flours, like brown and white rice flours, cornstarch, tapioca flour and potato starch. Some contain small amounts of gums, like xanthan gum or guar gum, and others are a blend of high-protein flours like chickpea, millet, teff and amaranth. They each have different binding properties, weights and rising abilities, so it's very important to understand the type of flour you're about to buy to make sure it syncs with your recipe.

Purchasing Gluten-Free All-Purpose Flour Blends

There are dozens of gluten-free all-purpose flours available in grocery stores all over the world. Picking the right one can often be a challenge. Over the years, our *Delight Gluten-Free Magazine* staff has tested more than fifty different flour blends and found them all to work rather differently, even in the exact same recipe! So how do we deal with that?

We always look for a flour blend that has a variety of ingredients to make a balanced mix. We like a blending of high-starch flours, high-protein flours and those that help keep baked goods moist. The blends we use must contain xanthan gum or guar gum as a binder. Without the added gum, you must buy a separate gum and add it yourself, which we feel defeats the purpose of purchasing an "all-purpose flour."

For the recipes throughout this book that use a gluten-free all-purpose flour, we have tested the recipes using the following brands of all-purpose flour blends: Better Batter, 1-2-3 Gluten Free, Pamela's Products and Glutino's Gluten-Free Pantry. Each of these all-purpose mixes contains different ingredients; however, the weights, properties and gums are all generally similar in nature and offer bakers an easy substitution between blends.

Making Your Own Gluten-Free Blend

If you're a total foodie or just one of those people who likes to maintain complete control in the kitchen, making your own gluten-free all-purpose blend might be the right way to go. If you choose this method, always make large batches ahead of time and store them in an airtight container so that at a moment's notice you have all-purpose flour to use. You never know when you may need to make an impromptu batch of chocolate chip cookies!

Below are three blends that *Delight* frequently uses that do not appear on any store shelves. They are blends we've developed over the years and use interchangeably in recipes.

Delight's Basic Gluten-Free All-Purpose Flour Blend

This is a starchy flour blend that's super-easy to make and is one of the cheaper all-purpose blends you'll find. The ingredients are easily purchased in most mainstream grocery stores. Simply blend the four ingredients together and store in an airtight container for up to one month. Use as a one-to-one replacement for all-purpose flour in baked goods recipes.

4 cups brown rice flour

1½ cups cornstarch

¼ cup tapioca flour

2 teaspoons xanthan or guar gum

Delight's High Protein and Fiber All-Purpose Blend

The sweet white sorghum flour brings protein, iron, antioxidants and dietary fiber to this nutrient-packed flour blend. The tapioca will add a thin and sturdy crust to your baked goods, and the coconut flour offers a distinctive and slightly sweet moistness. Simply blend using a stand mixer or whisk the four ingredients together and store in an airtight container for up to one month. Use as a one-to-one replacement for all-purpose flour in baked goods recipes.

3 cups sweet white sorghum flour

3 cups tapioca flour

1 cup coconut flour

3 teaspoons xanthan or guar gum

Delight's High-Protein, Low-Glycemic All-Purpose Blend

This flour blend is great for bakers looking to cut down on carbohydrates, but boost their protein intake. Buckwheat flour—which is actually the seed of a plant—contains more protein than rice, millet or corn and is packed with essential amino acids. The high levels of protein help to stabilize blood sugar levels, making it great for people on a low-glycemic diet. Almond flour is naturally low in carbohydrates and adds even more protein to this wonderful blend. Simply blend the four ingredients together and store in an airtight container for up to one month. Use as a one-to-one replacement for all-purpose flour in baked goods recipes, specifically quick breads and cakes, like carrot or apple cake.

3 cups buckwheat flour

2 cups almond flour

½ cup coconut flour

2 teaspoons xanthan or guar gum

Reading and Understanding Recipes

How *Delight*'s Test Kitchen Tests a Recipe

It's always an adventure working with a new recipe or ingredient. Sometimes we know the exact formula we want to use, while other times it's a puzzle that we assemble piece by piece. Our staff and contributors methodically put the recipes together, and then we test them to work out all the kinks.

Every recipe featured in the pages of *Delight Gluten-Free Magazine* and in this cookbook gets tested three times, even if it comes out perfectly the first time. We test all baked goods with at least three different gluten-free all-purpose flours because not all gluten-free flours are created equal. They have different binding properties, weights and rising abilities, so it's extremely important to have a recipe that adapts to any gluten-free flour a baker might use. We also test our recipes with different styles of baking equipment, including baking sheets, muffin tins, bundt pans, loaf pans, glass baking dishes and metal baking trays to ensure proper cooking times for whatever style of baked goods one wants to make.

The Anatomy of a Recipe

A recipe can take on many shapes and forms. At *Delight,* there are certain standards we follow for every single recipe we print to make sure the at-home cook has the same perfect results that we do in our test kitchen. See illustration on page 17 for how a recipe should look.

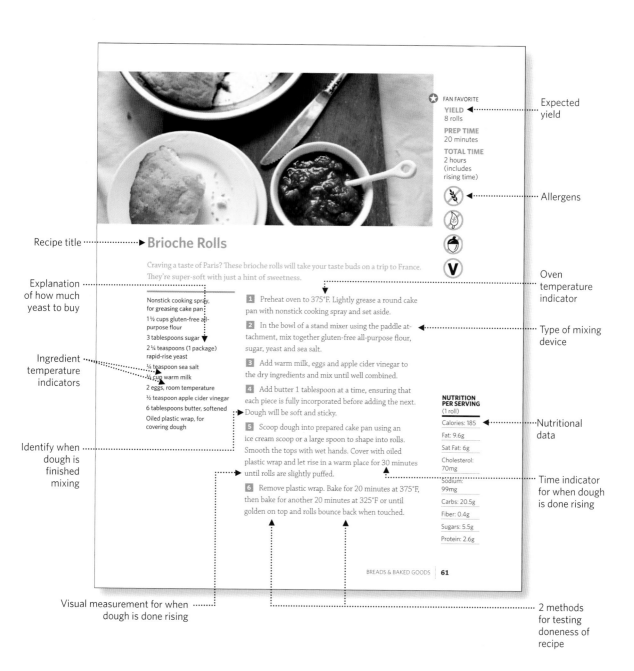

Recipe title ·······▶ **Brioche Rolls**

Expected yield

FAN FAVORITE

YIELD
8 rolls

PREP TIME
20 minutes

TOTAL TIME
2 hours
(includes
rising time)

Allergens

Craving a taste of Paris? These brioche rolls will take your taste buds on a trip to France. They're super-soft with just a hint of sweetness.

Explanation of how much yeast to buy

Ingredient temperature indicators

Identify when dough is finished mixing

Nonstick cooking spray, for greasing cake pan
1½ cups gluten-free all-purpose flour
3 tablespoons sugar
2¼ teaspoons (1 package) rapid-rise yeast
¼ teaspoon sea salt
¼ cup warm milk
2 eggs, room temperature
½ teaspoon apple cider vinegar
6 tablespoons butter, softened
Oiled plastic wrap, for covering dough

1 Preheat oven to 375°F. Lightly grease a round cake pan with nonstick cooking spray and set aside.

2 In the bowl of a stand mixer using the paddle attachment, mix together gluten-free all-purpose flour, sugar, yeast and sea salt.

3 Add warm milk, eggs and apple cider vinegar to the dry ingredients and mix until well combined.

4 Add butter 1 tablespoon at a time, ensuring that each piece is fully incorporated before adding the next. Dough will be soft and sticky.

5 Scoop dough into prepared cake pan using an ice cream scoop or a large spoon to shape into rolls. Smooth the tops with wet hands. Cover with oiled plastic wrap and let rise in a warm place for 30 minutes until rolls are slightly puffed.

6 Remove plastic wrap. Bake for 20 minutes at 375°F, then bake for another 20 minutes at 325°F or until golden on top and rolls bounce back when touched.

Oven temperature indicator

Type of mixing device

NUTRITION PER SERVING
(1 roll)

Calories: 185
Fat: 9.6g
Sat Fat: 6g
Cholesterol: 70mg
Sodium: 99mg
Carbs: 20.5g
Fiber: 0.4g
Sugars: 5.5g
Protein: 2.6g

Nutritional data

Time indicator for when dough is done rising

Visual measurement for when dough is done rising

2 methods for testing doneness of recipe

Allergens and Substitutions Guide

Every recipe in *Delight Gluten-Free Magazine* and in this cookbook is tagged with an allergen statement that tells users what common allergens the recipe is free of. Of course, every recipe is gluten-free, but we also address dairy, eggs, soy, nuts, rice and corn, as well, as if the recipe is vegetarian. Below are the icons you will see throughout the book that identify each allergen.

Gluten-Free Dairy-Free Egg-Free Soy-Free Nut-Free Rice-Free Corn-Free Vegetarian

Many people who require a gluten-free diet also have other food allergies or sensitivities. The most common requests we get at *Delight* are for recipes free of dairy and eggs. To help make all our recipes accessible to everyone, we've put together a quick guide for substituting both dairy and eggs in our recipes (see below).

Dairy Substitutes

Whether you're on a vegan diet, are lactose intolerant or gave up cow's milk for other health reasons, here are a few substitutes for dairy in your favorite recipes.

* **Milk Replacements:** soymilk, almond milk, rice milk, oat milk, hemp milk or coconut milk.

* **Sour Cream/Yogurt Replacements:** puréed silken tofu, applesauce, coconut yogurt, soy yogurt or almond yogurt.

* **Cheese Replacements:** soy cheese, rice cheese or almond cheese. Be sure to check cheese labels for casein. Many cheeses are lactose-free, but still contain casein, which is the protein in milk.

* **Butter/Margarine Replacements:** olive oil, canola oil, vegetable oil, coconut oil or applesauce. Use ¾ cup of these oils for every 1 cup of butter.

Egg Substitutes

Egg replacers can help leaven, bind and moisten your favorite recipes. Here are some of our most tried-and-true substitutions.

To Leaven

* Add 2 tablespoons lemon juice to wet ingredients and 1 teaspoon baking soda to dry ingredients

* ¼ teaspoon xanthan gum plus ¼ cup water

* 1 tablespoon agar agar powder plus 1 tablespoon water

To Bind

* 2 tablespoons cornstarch
* 1 tablespoon flax seeds plus 1 table-spoon water
* 1 ½ teaspoons tapioca starch plus ⅛ teaspoon xanthan gum plus 3 table-spoons water

To Moisten

* To replace 1 egg, use ¼ cup puréed banana, pear, pumpkin, sweet potato or applesauce
* If you need to moisten and leaven the baked good, add ¼ cup of desired purée plus ½ teaspoon baking powder

Trusted Brands and Resources

The gluten-free marketplace grows and expands almost daily, meaning that new products are always popping up on store shelves. Here are some of the brands that *Delight* uses most often in our test kitchen and we can verify that they taste great! These are just suggestions, so please feel free to select the brand that best fits your own personal nutritional needs.

Pasta (rice, corn or blend pastas)

* **DeLallo Gluten-Free Pasta** (gnocchi, elbows, orzo, spaghetti, penne, fusilli and shells)
* **Schar Gluten-Free Pasta** (tagliatelle, fusilli, anellini, spaghetti and penne)
* **Tinkyada Brown Rice Pasta** (spaghetti, spirals, penne, shells, fusilli, elbows, fettucini and lasagna)
* **Bionaturae Organic Gluten-Free Pasta** (fusilli, penne, elbows, rigatoni, linguine and spaghetti)
* **Heartland Gluten-Free Pasta** (penne, fusilli and spaghetti)
* **Probios Gluten-Free Pasta** (fusilli, spaghetti, maccheroncini, conchiglie, sedanini, penne and ditalini)
* **Ronzoni Gluten-Free Pasta** (penne, rotini and spaghetti)
* **Jovial Foods Gluten-Free Pasta** (spaghetti, capellini, penne, fusilli, caserecce, lasagna and tagliatelle)
* **Ancient Harvest** (elbows, linguine, spaghetti, rotelle and shells)
* **Glutino** (spaghetti, rotini, penne and macaroni)

Breadcrumbs

* **Glutino** (corn-based)
* **Schar** (rice-, corn- and soy-based)
* **Kinnikinnick** (tapioca- and rice-based)
* **Gillian's Foods** (rice-based)
* **Aleia's Italian Breadcrumbs** (corn-, rice- and tapioca-based)

Beers

- ★ **Bard's Beer** (craft beer brewed with sorghum)
- ★ **New Planet Beer** (pale ale, raspberry ale, amber ale and blonde ale)
- ★ **Dogfish Head Tweason'ale** (brewed with sorghum and strawberries)

Breads

- ★ **Schar** (baguettes, sandwich rolls, bagels, white bread and deli-style sliced breads)
- ★ **Against the Grain** (baguettes, rolls and bagels)
- ★ **Glutino** (white bread, flax seed bread, fiber bread, cinnamon-raisin bread, multigrain bread, English muffins and bagels)
- ★ **Rudi's Bakery** (multigrain bread, original bread, cinnamon-raisin bread, hamburger buns, hot dog buns and wraps)
- ★ **Udi's Gluten-Free Foods** (millet-chia bread, whole grain bread, white sandwich bread, cinnamon-raisin bread, flax and fiber bread, hamburger buns, hot dog buns, baguettes and French dinner rolls)
- ★ **Kinnikinnick** (white bread and multigrain bread)
- ★ **Food for Life** (multiseed English muffins and brown rice English muffins)
- ★ **French Meadow Bakery** (multigrain sandwich bread, white sandwich bread and cinnamon-raisin bread)

Crackers

- ★ **Crunchmaster** (multiseed, multigrain, rice and ancient grain)
- ★ **Glutino** (sea salt, rosemary & olive oil, original, cheddar, vegetable and multigrain)
- ★ **Ener-G** (table crackers)
- ★ **Schar** (table crackers)
- ★ **Blue Diamond** (nut thins)
- ★ **Mary's Gone Crackers** (super seed, onion and herb)
- ★ **Vans** (everything, cheese, roasted veggie and multigrain)

Graham Cracker Crumbs

- ★ **Kinnikinnick** (potato- and rice-based)
- ★ **Schar** (corn- and soy-based)

Soy Sauce and Fish Sauce

★ **San-J Tamari Sauce** (made from 100% soybeans—regular and low-sodium)

★ **Kikkoman Soy Sauce** (made from soybeans and rice)

★ **Eden Foods Organic Soy Sauce** (made from soybeans and rice)

★ **Thai Kitchen Fish Sauce** (made from salted anchovies)

Vegetable, Beef, Chicken and Seafood Stocks and Broths

★ **Massel Bouillon** (chicken, vegetable and beef stock)

★ **Imagine Foods** (chicken, vegetable and beef stock)

★ **Kitchen Basics** (chicken, vegetable, beef and seafood stock)

★ **Pacific Natural Foods** (chicken, beef and vegetable broths)

★ **Progresso** (chicken, beef and vegetable broths)

Gluten-Free Support Organizations

Celiac Disease Program at Children's National Medical Center **(www.childrensnational.org/celiac)**

University of Chicago Celiac Disease Center **(www.cureceliacdisease.org)**

Celiac Disease Foundation **(www.celiac.org)**

Gluten Intolerance Group **(www.gluten.net)**

CHAPTER TWO

Breads
& Baked
Goods

Raspberry Jelly-Filled Doughnuts – page 49

Peach Yogurt Quick Bread with Buttermilk Brandy Icing

YIELD
10 servings

PREP TIME
15 minutes

TOTAL TIME
1 hour
15 minutes

Quick bread is a type of bread that rises without the use of yeast, making it a fast and tasty breakfast option. The use of Greek yogurt in this recipe reduces the calorie count of the bread without taking away any of its delicious taste.

FOR THE PEACH YOGURT QUICK BREAD

Nonstick cooking spray, for greasing loaf pan

1 cup (2 sticks) butter, softened

¾ cup sugar

3 eggs, room temperature

⅓ cup plain Greek yogurt

2 ½ teaspoons vanilla extract

1 ½ cups gluten-free all-purpose flour

1 ½ teaspoons baking powder

½ teaspoon salt

2 cups diced peaches (about 2 large peaches)

FOR THE BUTTERMILK BRANDY ICING

1 cup powdered sugar

2 tablespoons peach brandy

1 tablespoon buttermilk

1. Preheat oven to 350°F. Spray a 9 x 5-inch loaf pan with nonstick cooking spray and set aside.

2. To make the peach yogurt quick bread, in the bowl of a stand mixer using the paddle attachment, cream together butter and sugar. Add eggs, 1 at a time, mixing well after each addition. Add Greek yogurt and vanilla extract and mix well.

3. In a separate bowl, whisk together gluten-free all-purpose flour, baking powder and salt. Slowly add dry ingredients into the wet ingredients, mixing well after each addition.

4. Gently fold in peaches and pour batter into prepared loaf pan. Bake for 50 to 60 minutes until a toothpick inserted into the center of the bread comes out clean. Cool on a wire rack for 10 minutes before icing.

5. To make the buttermilk brandy icing, whisk together powdered sugar, peach brandy and buttermilk.

6. Carefully remove cake from the pan and drizzle icing over top before slicing.

NUTRITION PER SERVING

Calories: 320

Fat: 18g

Sat Fat: 11g

Cholesterol: 95mg

Sodium: 320mg

Carbs: 37g

Fiber: 2g

Sugars: 25g

Protein: 4g

Honey Oat Loaf

This easy-to-make, slightly sweet quick bread goes perfectly with peanut butter, cream cheese or your favorite jam. The honey gives the bread a hint of sweetness without adding any artificial sweeteners. If you can't find oat flour that is certified gluten-free, purchase whole gluten-free oats and pulse them in a food processor to create your own homemade flour.

YIELD
12 servings

PREP TIME
15 minutes

TOTAL TIME
1 hour
10 minutes

FOR THE BREAD

Parchment paper, for lining loaf pan

1 cup gluten-free oat flour

½ cup blanched almond flour

¼ cup coconut flour

1 ½ teaspoons baking powder

½ teaspoon salt

4 eggs, room temperature, yolks and whites separated

2 tablespoons honey

1 cup nonfat milk

2 ½ teaspoons apple cider vinegar

FOR THE TOPPING

2 tablespoons butter, melted

2 tablespoons honey

¼ teaspoon salt

1 Preheat oven to 350°F. Line a 9 x 5-inch loaf pan with parchment paper, leaving a bit of overhang on the sides, and set aside.

2 To make the bread, in a large bowl, combine oat flour, almond flour, coconut flour, baking powder and salt. Whisk to combine.

3 In a separate bowl, beat together egg yolks, honey, milk and apple cider vinegar.

4 In the bowl of a stand mixer using the whisk attachment or using a hand mixer, whip egg whites until stiff peaks form.

5 Add egg yolk mixture into the dry ingredients and beat to combine. Gently fold in egg whites until fully combined. Pour batter into prepared loaf pan.

6 Bake for 50 to 55 minutes until bread springs back when touched and a toothpick inserted into the center of the bread comes out clean.

7 To make the topping, in a small bowl, whisk together melted butter, honey and salt. Brush topping mixture on top of bread as soon as it comes out of the oven.

8 Let bread cool on a wire rack for 10 minutes, then remove from pan and continue cooling. Cool completely before slicing.

NUTRITION PER SERVING

Calories: 140

Fat: 7g

Sat Fat: 2.5g

Cholesterol: 80mg

Sodium: 270mg

Carbs: 14g

Fiber: 2g

Sugars: 7g

Protein: 5g

Currant & Caraway Soda Bread

YIELD
8 servings

PREP TIME
20 minutes

TOTAL TIME
50 to 60 minutes

This soda bread is a hardy, dense bread that is lightened with the flavors of currants and caraway seeds. If you can't find currants, use regular or golden raisins instead.

Parchment paper, for lining baking sheet

3 cups gluten-free all-purpose flour, plus additional for kneading the dough

2 tablespoons sugar

1 tablespoon caraway seeds

2 teaspoons baking soda

¾ teaspoon salt

¾ cup currants

1 cup Greek yogurt, plain, 2% or full fat

¼ cup milk

1 whole egg

2 egg yolks

1 Preheat oven to 375°F. Line a baking sheet with parchment paper and set aside.

2 In a large bowl, whisk together gluten-free all-purpose flour, sugar, caraway seeds, baking soda and salt. Add currants to the dry ingredients, using your fingers to separate the fruit from itself if individual pieces are stuck together, and toss with flour.

3 In a separate large bowl, combine Greek yogurt, milk, egg and egg yolks. Add wet ingredients into the dry ingredients and use a rubber spatula to combine.

4 Sprinkle a tablespoon or 2 of gluten-free all-purpose flour onto the kitchen counter or cutting board. Place dough onto floured surface and knead into an 8-inch diameter round loaf. Using a knife cut a ½-inch deep "X" across the top of the bread.

5 Place bread on the parchment-lined baking sheet and bake for 30 to 40 minutes. Bread is finished baking when it is browned and sounds hollow when tapped.

6 Remove bread from oven and place on a cooling rack. Serve warm or at room temperature.

NUTRITION PER SERVING

Calories: 290

Fat: 1.5g

Sat Fat: 1.5g

Cholesterol: 100mg

Sodium: 740mg

Carbs: 53g

Fiber: 7g

Sugars: 8g

Protein: 12g

YIELD
10 servings

PREP TIME
10 minutes

TOTAL TIME
1 hour

Lemon Poppy Seed Loaf

This sweet citrus loaf is packed with real lemon juice and zest, giving it a tart bite. If you're up for a bit of a new flavor profile, try adding ¼ teaspoon of ground ginger to the frosting.

NUTRITION PER SERVING

Calories: 420

Fat: 20g

Sat Fat: 2g

Cholesterol: 80mg

Sodium: 390mg

Carbs: 59g

Fiber: 2g

Sugars: 41g

Protein: 5g

FOR THE LOAF BREAD

Nonstick cooking spray, for greasing loaf pan

1½ cups gluten-free all-purpose flour

1 teaspoon baking powder

1 teaspoon salt

3 eggs

1 cup sugar

½ cup plus 2 tablespoons canola or vegetable oil

1 teaspoon vanilla extract

¼ cup plus 2 tablespoons fresh lemon juice

Zest of 2 lemons

2 teaspoons poppy seeds

FOR THE GLAZE

1 cup powdered sugar

2 tablespoons fresh lemon juice, plus more if desired

1 teaspoon lemon zest

1 Preheat oven to 350°F. Spray an 8 x 4-inch loaf pan with nonstick cooking spray and set aside.

2 To make the loaf bread, in a mixing bowl, whisk together gluten-free all-purpose flour, baking powder and salt.

3 In the bowl of a stand mixer using the paddle attachment, beat together eggs, sugar, canola or vegetable oil, vanilla extract, lemon juice and lemon zest. Add dry ingredients in 3 separate additions, mixing well after each addition. Add poppy seeds and mix well.

4 Pour batter into prepared loaf pan and bake for 45 to 50 minutes until a toothpick inserted into the center of the loaf comes out clean. Cool on a wire rack for 10 minutes before icing.

5 To make the glaze, whisk together powdered sugar, lemon juice and lemon zest. Pour glaze over the loaf and continue cooling.

YIELD
10 servings

PREP TIME
20 minutes

TOTAL TIME
1 hour
20 minutes

Chai Spiced Zucchini Bread

Chai tea latte meets zucchini bread in this naturally gluten-free quick bread. Because of its high water content, zucchini bread is naturally extra moist, but in this case, the added Greek yogurt keeps the bread super-soft even longer. Gone are the days of crumbly gluten-free breads!

Nonstick cooking spray, for greasing loaf pan

1 cup sorghum flour

½ cup cornstarch

½ cup coconut flour

1 teaspoon ground cinnamon

1 teaspoon ground ginger

½ teaspoon allspice

½ teaspoon baking powder

½ teaspoon salt

½ cup granulated sugar

½ cup brown sugar

¾ cup canola or coconut oil

½ cup plain Greek yogurt

2 eggs

1 teaspoon vanilla extract

1½ cups shredded zucchini

1 Preheat oven to 350°F. Lightly grease an 8 x 4-inch loaf pan with nonstick cooking spray and set aside.

2 In a mixing bowl, whisk together sorghum flour, cornstarch, coconut flour, cinnamon, ginger, allspice, baking powder and salt.

3 In the bowl of a stand mixer using the paddle attachment, beat together granulated sugar, brown sugar, canola or coconut oil, Greek yogurt, eggs and vanilla extract. Mix until thick and smooth.

4 Add dry ingredients into the wet ingredients in 3 separate additions, beating well after each addition.
Fold in zucchini.

5 Pour batter into prepared loaf pan and bake for 55 to 60 minutes until a toothpick inserted into the center of the bread comes out clean. Cool before removing from the pan and slicing.

NUTRITION PER SERVING

Calories: 440

Fat: 25g

Sat Fat: 4g

Cholesterol: 55mg

Sodium: 220mg

Carbs: 50g

Fiber: 4g

Sugars: 26g

Protein: 6g

Chocolate Chip Apple Bread

Most kids will beg for chocolate at all hours of the day, and this quick bread will satisfy your little one's cravings. But if chocolate isn't your thing, substitute dried fruit, raisins or yogurt chips for a lightened loaf.

Nonstick cooking spray, for greasing loaf pan

1 ½ cups gluten-free all-purpose flour

2 teaspoons ground cinnamon

1 teaspoon baking powder

½ teaspoon salt

¼ teaspoon nutmeg

1 cup sugar

2 eggs

¼ cup canola oil

¼ cup applesauce

1 teaspoon vanilla extract

2 cups shredded green apples

¾ cup semisweet chocolate chips

1 Preheat oven to 350°F. Spray an 8 x 4-inch loaf pan with nonstick cooking spray and set aside.

2 In a large mixing bowl, whisk together gluten-free all-purpose flour, cinnamon, baking powder, salt and nutmeg.

3 In the bowl of a stand mixer using the paddle attachment, beat together sugar, eggs, canola oil, applesauce and vanilla extract. In 3 separate additions, add dry ingredients, mixing well after each addition. Add apples and mix well.

4 Fold in chocolate chips and pour batter into prepared loaf pan. Bake for 52 to 55 minutes until golden and a toothpick inserted into the center of the loaf comes out clean. Cool before removing from pan and slicing.

NUTRITION PER SERVING

Calories: 360

Fat: 14g

Sat Fat: 4g

Cholesterol: 55mg

Sodium: 90mg

Carbs: 59g

Fiber: 4g

Sugars: 39g

Protein: 5g

YIELD
10 servings

PREP TIME
15 minutes

TOTAL TIME
1 hour

Caramelized Banana Bread with Brown Butter Glaze

This dense and sturdy bread gets its deep rich flavor from caramelized bananas and a glaze infused with golden browned butter. If your pantry isn't stocked with these specialty flours, feel free to replace the brown rice flour, oat flour, sorghum flour, potato starch and xanthan gum with 2 cups of a gluten-free all-purpose flour. Just make sure the flour you select contains xanthan or guar gum.

FOR THE BANANA BREAD

Nonstick cooking spray, for greasing loaf pan

3 tablespoons butter

¾ cup brown sugar

3 very ripe bananas, sliced

2 eggs

½ cup plus 1 teaspoon milk, divided

3 tablespoons coconut oil, melted

1 teaspoon vanilla extract

1 cup potato starch

½ cup brown rice flour

¼ cup gluten-free oat flour

¼ cup sorghum flour

1 teaspoon xanthan gum

1 teaspoon baking powder

1 teaspoon ground cinnamon

½ teaspoon allspice

½ teaspoon salt

FOR THE BROWN BUTTER GLAZE

3 tablespoons butter

⅓ cup powdered sugar

1 tablespoon milk

1 Preheat oven to 350°F. Lightly grease a loaf pan with nonstick cooking spray and set aside.

2 To make the banana bread, in a small skillet, melt butter over medium-high heat. Once butter is melted, add brown sugar and whisk to combine. Add bananas and cook for 4 to 5 minutes until bananas begin to caramelize.

3 Remove banana mixture from heat. In the bowl of a stand mixer using the paddle attachment, add banana mixture and beat until very smooth.

4 In a separate bowl, whisk together eggs, milk, melted coconut oil and vanilla extract.

5 In a large bowl, combine potato starch, brown rice flour, oat flour, sorghum flour, xanthan gum, baking powder, cinnamon, allspice and salt. Whisk to combine.

6 Add milk mixture and flour mixture to bananas in 3 additions, alternating between milk and flour. Beat until just combined.

7 Pour batter into prepared loaf pan and bake for 40 to 50 minutes until a toothpick inserted into the center of the bread comes out clean. Let cool in pan for 15 minutes, then remove bread from pan and finish cooling on a baking rack.

8 To make the brown butter glaze, melt butter in a skillet over medium heat. Butter will begin to turn golden brown. Once butter has turned a deep golden color, remove from heat and add powdered sugar and milk, whisking constantly. Add more milk to achieve a drippy but thick texture, if necessary. Pour glaze over the cooled bread.

NUTRITION PER SERVING

Calories: 420

Fat: 16g

Sat Fat: 10g

Cholesterol: 80mg

Sodium: 320mg

Carbs: 68g

Fiber: 3g

Sugars: 29g

Protein: 4g

YIELD
10 servings

PREP TIME
15 minutes

TOTAL TIME
6 hours
30 minutes
(includes
cashew soak-
ing time)

**NUTRITION
PER SERVING**

Calories: 740

Fat: 47g

Sat Fat: 29g

Cholesterol:
160mg

Sodium:
640mg

Carbs: 72g

Fiber: 6g

Sugars: 49g

Protein: 12g

Carrot Cake Bread
with Cashew Cream Frosting

This cake-like quick bread is covered with a delicious dairy-free cashew cream frosting, making it a healthy alternative to a traditional carrot cake. The carrots, pineapple and coconut flakes help keep the bread moist for days, assuming you don't eat it all in one sitting! If you want to make this recipe and don't have time to let the cashews soak, replace the cashew frosting with any dairy-free frosting of your choice.

FOR THE CARROT CAKE BREAD

Nonstick cooking spray
or coconut oil, for
greasing loaf pan

6 eggs

1 cup coconut oil, melted

1 cup honey

2 teaspoons vanilla extract

¾ cup buckwheat flour

½ cup almond flour

¼ cup coconut flour

2 teaspoons baking powder

2 teaspoons
ground cinnamon

1 teaspoon salt

2 cups shredded carrots

½ cup canned diced
pineapple, drained

⅓ cup shredded
unsweetened coconut flakes

¼ cup slivered almonds plus
extra for garnish

Foli, for covering loaf pan

FOR THE CASHEW CREAM
FROSTING

1 cup raw unsalted cashews

⅓–½ cup almond milk

⅓ cup honey

2 teaspoons vanilla extract

Pinch of salt

1 Place raw unsalted cashews in a bowl of water and soak for up to 6 hours in the refrigerator.

2 Preheat oven to 300°F. Lightly grease a loaf pan with nonstick cooking spray or coconut oil and set aside.

3 To make the carrot cake bread, in the bowl of a stand mixer using the paddle attachment, combine eggs, melted coconut oil, honey and vanilla extract. Beat on medium speed until well combined.

4 In a separate bowl, whisk together buckwheat flour, almond flour, coconut flour, baking powder, cinnamon and salt.

5 Add flour mixture to the egg mixture in 3 additions, beating well between each addition.

6 With the mixer running on low speed, add carrots, pineapple, coconut flakes and almonds. Mix just until combined.

7 Pour batter into prepared loaf pan and bake for 1 hour uncovered. Cover loaf pan with foil and bake an additional 25 to 30 minutes until a toothpick inserted into the center of the bread comes out clean. Let cool in pan for 15 minutes, then remove bread from pan and finish cooling on a baking rack.

8 To make cashew cream frosting, place soaked cashews, almond milk, honey, vanilla extract and salt in a blender. Blend on high speed until very smooth. Add additional milk, if needed.

9 Place frosting in refrigerator until it is fully chilled. Lightly frost bread with the chilled frosting and top with additional slivered almonds.

YIELD
10 servings

PREP TIME
15 minutes

TOTAL TIME
2 hours
(includes
rising time)

Monkey Bread

This monkey bread truly tastes like the real thing. It's a sweet treat that is perfect for a gathering of family and friends or just a weekend brunch! If you want to spice up this basic recipe, toss a handful of chopped pecans and golden raisins into the dough.

FOR THE BREAD

Butter and parchment paper, for greasing pan and baking sheets

2 ½ cups gluten-free all-purpose flour, plus additional for rolling out

½ teaspoon salt

2 eggs

4 tablespoons (½ stick) butter, room temperature

2 ¼ teaspoons (1 packet) rapid-rise yeast

¼ cup sugar

¾ cup warm milk

FOR THE GLAZE

1 cup brown sugar

2 tablespoons ground cinnamon

8 tablespoons (1 stick) butter

1 Preheat oven to 375°F. Line 2 baking sheets with parchment paper and set aside. Lightly grease a springform pan with butter and set aside.

2 To make the bread, in the bowl of a stand mixer using the paddle attachment, combine gluten-free all-purpose flour and salt. Gently mix to combine. Add eggs and butter, beating on medium speed until fully incorporated. Add yeast and sugar and beat again to combine.

3 Gently stream in warm milk while mixing on low until dough begins to come together. Beat for another 2 to 3 minutes on high speed. The dough should be sticky. If it appears too smooth or dry, add additional milk.

4 Turn dough out onto a lightly floured surface and pat into a 1-inch-thick square. Cut dough into 36 equal-sized pieces and roll pieces into balls.

5 Place balls of dough on prepared baking sheets and cover with a kitchen towel. Let rise in a warm area for 1 hour or until dough has roughly doubled in size.

6 To make the glaze, in a mixing bowl, combine brown sugar and cinnamon and whisk well to combine. Dredge each ball of dough through cinnamon and sugar mixture and place in prepared springform pan in a circular pattern, staggering dough balls and squeezing them close together. Pour remaining cinnamon and sugar mixture over dough balls.

7 Melt butter in a separate dish and pour over dough balls in the pan. Place pan on a baking sheet lined with foil and bake for 35 to 40 minutes until a toothpick inserted into the center of the bread comes out clean—ignore gooey topping, you're just looking for the bread part to be cooked through.

8 Let cool in pan for 5 to 7 minutes, then run a knife around the edges and carefully release bread from the pan. Invert pan onto a plate or cake stand. Serve warm.

**NUTRITION
PER SERVING**

Calories: 430

Fat: 20g

Sat Fat: 11g

Cholesterol: 100mg

Sodium: 330mg

Carbs: 61g

Fiber: 5g

Sugars: 33g

Protein: 7g

Pumpkin Spice Cream Cheese Swirl Muffins

Pumpkin pie meets cheesecake in these swirly muffins. This morning goody manages to take the sweetness of the pumpkin spice and the moistness of the cream cheese to make a rich cake-like muffin your entire family will enjoy.

FOR THE CREAM CHEESE FILLING

Nonstick cooking spray or oil, for greasing muffin tin

8 ounces cream cheese, softened

1 egg

4 tablespoons sugar

½ teaspoon vanilla extract

FOR THE MUFFIN BATTER

½ cup finely ground almond flour

½ cup cornstarch

¼ cup brown rice flour

¼ cup sorghum flour

3 teaspoons baking powder

1 teaspoon pumpkin pie spice

½ teaspoon salt

¼ teaspoon nutmeg

1 cup granulated sugar

1 cup pumpkin purée

¼ cup melted butter, slightly cooled

2 tablespoons maple syrup

2 eggs, room temperature

1 teaspoon vanilla extract

1 Preheat oven to 350°F. Lightly grease a muffin tin with nonstick cooking spray or oil and set aside.

2 To make the cream cheese filling, in the bowl of a stand mixer using the paddle attachment, combine cream cheese, egg, sugar and vanilla extract. Beat until thick and creamy. Transfer to a small bowl and refrigerate until ready to use.

3 To make the muffin batter, in a large bowl, whisk together almond flour, cornstarch, brown rice flour, sorghum flour, baking powder, pumpkin pie spice, salt and nutmeg.

4 In the bowl of a stand mixer using the paddle attachment, combine sugar, pumpkin purée, melted butter, maple syrup, eggs and vanilla extract. Beat until thoroughly combined.

5 Add dry ingredients into the wet ingredients in 3 additions, beating until fully incorporated between each addition.

6 Fill each muffin tin halfway full, then evenly distribute cream cheese filling on top of the batter. Top batter and cream cheese filling in each of the muffin tins evenly with remaining batter and then swirl each muffin gently with a butter knife.

7 Bake for 30 to 35 minutes until a toothpick inserted into the center of the muffins comes out clean. Cool in muffin tin for 5 minutes, then finish cooling on cooling rack.

**NUTRITION
PER SERVING**
(1 muffin)

Calories: 290

Fat: 14g

Sat Fat: 7g

Cholesterol: 85mg

Sodium: 350mg

Carbs: 37g

Fiber: 2g

Sugars: 25g

Protein: 5g

YIELD
12 muffins

PREP TIME
10 minutes

TOTAL TIME
35 minutes

Blueberry Crumble Muffins

Kick off your morning with these light and fresh blueberry muffins. If you have fresh blueberries on hand, feel free to use them instead of the frozen blueberries.

FOR THE MUFFIN BATTER

Paper liners and nonstick cooking spray, for greasing muffin tin

2 cups gluten-free all-purpose flour

2 teaspoons baking powder

1 teaspoon salt

1 cup sugar

½ cup vegetable oil

2 eggs

⅓ cup milk

¼ cup lemon juice

1 teaspoon lemon zest

1 cup frozen blueberries

FOR THE CRUMB TOPPING

¼ cup sugar

⅛ cup cornstarch

2 tablespoons butter, cut into small pieces

Zest of 1 lemon

1 Preheat oven to 375°F. Line a muffin tin with paper liners and lightly spray with nonstick cooking spray and set aside.

2 To make the muffin batter, in a mixing bowl, whisk together gluten-free all-purpose flour, baking powder and salt.

3 In the bowl of a stand mixer using the paddle attachment, cream together sugar, vegetable oil, eggs, milk, lemon juice and lemon zest. Beat until light and smooth.

4 Add dry ingredients into the wet ingredients in 3 separate additions, making sure to mix well after each addition. Fold in the blueberries.

5 To make the crumb topping, in a small bowl, mix together sugar, cornstarch, butter and lemon zest until small pea-sized crumbles form.

6 Pour batter evenly into prepared muffin tin. Sprinkle crumb topping evenly across each of the muffins. Bake for 25 to 28 minutes until a toothpick inserted into the center of the muffins comes out clean. Cool in muffin tin for 5 minutes, then finish cooling on cooling rack.

NUTRITION PER SERVING
(1 muffin)

Calories: 270

Fat: 13g

Sat Fat: 2g

Cholesterol: 40mg

Sodium: 320mg

Carbs: 40g

Fiber: 2g

Sugars: 23g

Protein: 3g

Cinnamon Swirl Applesauce Muffins

These muffins pair perfectly with a cup of coffee as a morning treat or an afternoon pick-me-up. If you're looking to add some quality soluble fiber to these muffins, try using ¼ cup gluten-free all-purpose flour and ¼ cup gluten-free quick-cook oats in the streusel topping. The oats add a hearty nutritional punch and great texture!

YIELD
12 muffins

PREP TIME
15 minutes

TOTAL TIME
45 minutes

FOR THE STREUSEL TOPPING

Butter or nonstick cooking spray, for greasing muffin tin

½ cup gluten-free all-purpose flour

½ cup brown sugar

¼ teaspoon salt

3 tablespoons cold butter, cut into cubes

FOR THE MUFFIN BATTER

1 ½ cups gluten-free all-purpose flour

3 teaspoons baking powder

1 teaspoon ground cinnamon

½ teaspoon salt

½ cup plain yogurt

½ cup applesauce

8 tablespoons (1 stick) butter, room temperature

½ cup sugar

1 teaspoon vanilla extract

2 eggs

1 To make the streusel topping, in a mixing bowl, combine gluten-free all-purpose flour, brown sugar and salt. Cut in butter with a fork until mixture forms large, coarse crumbs. Refrigerate until ready to use.

2 Preheat oven to 350°F. Lightly grease a muffin tin with butter or nonstick cooking spray and set aside.

3 To make the muffin batter, in a medium bowl, whisk together gluten-free all-purpose flour, baking powder, cinnamon and salt.

4 In the bowl of a stand mixer using the paddle attachment or using an electric mixer and a bowl, beat together yogurt, applesauce, butter, sugar and vanilla extract until very light and creamy. Add eggs, 1 at a time, mixing well between each addition.

5 Add dry ingredients into the wet ingredients in 3 additions, beating on low until just combined between each addition.

6 Place half the batter in each muffin tin, filling each one less than halfway full. Sprinkle with half the streusel topping, then top with remaining batter. Top muffins with remaining streusel topping.

7 Bake for 25 to 30 minutes until a toothpick inserted into the center of the muffins comes out clean. Cool in muffin tin for 5 minutes, then finish cooling on cooling rack.

NUTRITION PER SERVING
(1 muffin)

Calories: 330

Fat: 16g

Sat Fat: 10g

Cholesterol: 80mg

Sodium: 400mg

Carbs: 44g

Fiber: 3g

Sugars: 26g

Protein: 4g

Chocolate Almond Apricot Scones

These almond flour–based scones are a great grain-free alternative to the traditional breakfast treat. The combination of apricot and chocolate chips provides some sweetness that contrasts nicely with the nutty almond flavor.

Silicon mat or parchment paper, for lining baking sheet

2 cups almond flour

¾ teaspoon baking powder

½ teaspoon salt

4 tablespoons (½ stick) cold butter, cut into cubes

2 eggs

3 tablespoons honey

½ teaspoon vanilla extract

½ cup chocolate chips

½ cup diced, dried apricots

1 Preheat oven to 350°F. Line a baking sheet with a silicon mat or lightly greased parchment paper and set aside.

2 In a large bowl, combine almond flour, baking powder and salt. Whisk to combine.

3 Cut butter into flour mixture using a fork until mixture resembles large, coarse grains of sand.

4 In a separate bowl, whisk together eggs, honey and vanilla extract. Add egg mixture to flour mixture and gently stir together with a fork until combined.

5 Fold in chocolate chips and dried apricots. Knead dough with hands if necessary to evenly distribute.

6 Turn dough out onto baking sheet and form into a ½-inch-thick circle. Cut dough into 8 slices and gently separate each slice. You can place them on a different baking sheet or rearrange them as desired.

7 Bake for 15 to 20 minutes until golden brown. Let cool on baking sheet for 2 to 3 minutes. Serve warm.

NUTRITION PER SERVING
(1 scone)

Calories: 330

Fat: 24g

Sat Fat: 7g

Cholesterol: 70mg

Sodium: 280mg

Carbs: 25g

Fiber: 4g

Sugars: 17g

Protein: 8g

YIELD
8 scones

PREP TIME
5 minutes

TOTAL TIME
30 minutes

Lemon Thyme Scones

These traditional biscuit-like scones are enhanced with the flavors of lemon and dried thyme. For an added boost of nutrients, add a handful of chopped dried apricots.

FOR THE SCONES

Parchment paper and nonstick cooking spray, for lining and greasing baking sheet

2 cups gluten-free all-purpose flour

⅓ cup sugar

2 teaspoons baking powder

¼ teaspoon salt

8 tablespoons (1 stick) cold butter, cut into cubes

½ cup cold buttermilk

2 teaspoons lemon zest

½ teaspoon dried thyme

FOR THE SUGAR TOPPING

¼ cup sugar

2 teaspoons lemon zest

1 Preheat oven to 350°F. Line a baking sheet with parchment paper and spray with nonstick cooking spray and set aside.

2 To make the scones, in a bowl, mix together gluten-free all-purpose flour, sugar, baking powder and salt until well combined.

3 Cut in butter using a pastry blender or fork until small pea-sized crumbles form. Add buttermilk, lemon zest and thyme and mix until well combined.

4 Using your hands, shape dough into a large ball. Press out dough on prepared baking sheet into a circle that is approximately 8 inches in diameter.

5 Using a sharp knife, cut dough into 8 wedges, but do not cut completely apart.

6 To make the sugar topping, in a separate small bowl, whisk together sugar and lemon zest. Sprinkle lemon sugar on top of the prepared dough. Bake for 22 to 25 minutes until lightly golden. Cool slightly and pull scones apart to serve.

NUTRITION PER SERVING
(1 scone)

Calories: 270

Fat: 13g

Sat Fat: 8g

Cholesterol: 30mg

Sodium: 330mg

Carbs: 38g

Fiber: 3g

Sugars: 16g

Protein: 4g

Bacon Cheddar Scones

YIELD
8 scones

PREP TIME
15 minutes

TOTAL TIME
40 minutes

These scones make a delicious addition to the brunch table. You can even make the dough the night before then simply shape, cut and bake when it's time to serve! Plus, what on earth could be better than baked goods with bacon? Want to sweeten the bite? Drizzle Maple syrup on top of the warm scones.

Silicon mat or parchment paper, for lining baking sheet

4 slices bacon

1 cup brown rice flour

½ cup sorghum flour

½ cup cornstarch

¼ cup millet flour

1 ½ teaspoons baking powder

1 teaspoon xanthan gum

1 teaspoon salt

1 teaspoon pepper

6 tablespoons cold butter, cut into cubes

1 cup buttermilk

2 eggs

1 cup shredded extra-sharp cheddar cheese

1 Preheat oven to 425°F. Line a baking sheet with a silicon mat or parchment paper and set aside.

2 Cook bacon in a skillet until fat is rendered and bacon is crispy. Drain on a paper towel–lined plate. Let cool, then dice into very small pieces and set aside.

3 In a large bowl, combine brown rice flour, sorghum flour, cornstarch, millet flour, baking powder, xanthan gum, salt and pepper. Whisk well to combine.

4 Cut butter into flour mixture using a fork until mixture resembles large, coarse crumbs.

5 In a separate small bowl, whisk together buttermilk and eggs. Add egg and buttermilk mixture to the flour mixture and combine with a fork.

6 Fold in the cheese and diced bacon. Form dough into a ½-inch-thick circle and cut out small rounds or cut into 8 equal triangular pieces.

7 Bake for 15 to 20 minutes or until lightly golden brown. Let cool on baking sheet for 5 minutes. Serve warm.

NUTRITION PER SERVING
(1 scone)

Calories: 380

Fat: 23g

Sat Fat: 11g

Cholesterol: 105mg

Sodium: 730mg

Carbs: 35g

Fiber: 2g

Sugars: 2g

Protein: 11g

PREP TIME
50 minutes

TOTAL TIME
1 hour
20 minutes
(includes
rising time)

Sparkling Cider Apple Fritters

Hands down one of the best gluten-free doughnuts you'll ever eat. With a puffy dough, sweetened by caramelized apples, these doughnuts are so good, you can't eat just one of them. The recipe yields 14 doughnuts that are a typical doughnut shop size. If you want to make more doughnuts from the same recipe, create doughnut hole–sized rounds instead of the larger rectangles.

FOR THE DOUGHNUT DOUGH

2 ¼ teaspoons (1 packet) rapid-rise yeast

¾ cup warm milk

2 whole eggs

2 egg yolks

½ cup sugar

¼ cup sparkling apple cider

4 tablespoons (½ stick) butter, melted

3 teaspoons vanilla extract

3 ½ cups gluten-free all-purpose flour, plus additional for rolling out

1 ½ teaspoons salt

1 teaspoon ground cinnamon

Plastic wrap, for covering dough

Canola oil for frying

FOR THE CARAMELIZED APPLES

3 tablespoons butter

¼ cup brown sugar

1 ½ teaspoons vanilla extract

1 teaspoon ground cinnamon

½ cup sparkling apple cider

1 tablespoon cider vinegar

5 cups finely chopped Granny Smith apples (about 4 apples)

FOR THE GLAZE

1 cup powdered sugar

½ cup sparkling apple cider

1 teaspoon vanilla extract

¾ teaspoon sea salt

½ teaspoon ground cinnamon

1 To make the doughnut dough, in the bowl of a stand mixer using the paddle attachment, combine yeast and warm milk. Let sit for about 5 minutes until the yeast has dissolved and becomes foamy.

2 To the yeast mixture, add whole eggs, egg yolks, sugar, sparkling apple cider, melted butter and vanilla extract. Mix until well combined.

3 In a separate bowl, whisk together gluten-free all-purpose flour, salt and cinnamon. Slowly add dry ingredients into the wet ingredients, mixing well after each addition. Mix until dough comes together in a smooth ball. Leave dough in the mixer bowl, cover with plastic wrap and let rise in a warm place for 25 to 30 minutes.

4 To make the caramelized apples, heat butter in a large skillet over medium-high heat. Add brown sugar, vanilla extract and cinnamon and stir constantly until sugar has dissolved. Reduce heat to medium and add sparkling apple cider and cider vinegar. Bring to a simmer and then add apples. Cook, stirring occasionally, until apples are soft and most of the liquid has evaporated and has become syrupy. Remove from heat and cool completely.

5 Once apples have cooled completely, transfer them to the bowl of the stand mixer with the dough. Using the paddle attachment on the lowest setting, gently mix apples into the dough. Dust a workspace with gluten-free all-purpose flour and roll dough out into a large ball. Divide dough ball into 14 equal-sized pieces and form into rough rectangles.

6 In a large Dutch oven or nonstick pot, heat approximately 3 inches of canola oil to 350°F. Drop doughnuts into the hot oil and fry for approximately 4 to 5 minutes per side until golden brown. Be careful not to overcrowd the pot of oil.

7 Once doughnuts are cooked, transfer them to a rack set on top of paper towels to drain excess oil. Repeat until all doughnuts are fried.

8 To make the glaze, whisk together powdered sugar, sparkling apple cider, vanilla extract, sea salt and cinnamon in a small saucepan over medium-low heat. Continue whisking over heat, just until glaze is warm. Brush glaze over each of the doughnuts before serving.

NUTRITION PER SERVING
(1 doughnut)

Calories: 430

Fat: 24g

Sat Fat: 7g

Cholesterol: 75mg

Sodium: 450mg

Carbs: 51g

Fiber: 4g

Sugars: 27g

Protein: 5g

Old-Fashioned Buttermilk Doughnuts

YIELD
8 doughnuts

PREP TIME
10 minutes

TOTAL TIME
25 minutes

A simple glaze tops these classic old-fashioned buttermilk doughnuts. While the recipe doesn't require you to cut out a center hole, if you feel the need to have an open center, go right ahead and cut it out!

FOR THE DOUGHNUT DOUGH

2 ¼ cups gluten-free all-purpose flour, plus additional for rolling out

1 teaspoon ground cinnamon

½ teaspoon nutmeg

1 teaspoon baking powder

½ teaspoon salt

1 egg

½ cup sugar

1 tablespoon butter, melted

¾ cup buttermilk

Canola oil, for frying

FOR THE GLAZE

1 cup powdered sugar

½ cup milk

1 teaspoon vanilla extract

½ teaspoon salt

1 To make the doughnut dough, in a large mixing bowl, whisk together gluten-free all-purpose flour, cinnamon, nutmeg, baking powder and salt.

2 In the bowl of a stand mixer, beat together egg, sugar, melted butter and buttermilk. Slowly add dry ingredients into these wet ingredients, mixing well after each addition. Mix until dough is smooth and pulls together.

3 Turn dough out onto a work surface dusted with gluten-free all-purpose flour. Roll dough into a 9-inch circle that is approximately ½ inch thick. Cut dough into 8 rounds using a biscuit cutter.

4 In a wide pot, heat approximately 2 inches of canola oil to 350°F. Drop doughnuts into the hot oil and fry for approximately 4 to 5 minutes per side until golden brown. Do not overcrowd the pot. Once cooked, remove doughnuts from the oil and transfer them to a rack set on top of paper towels to drain. Repeat until all doughnuts are fried.

5 To make the glaze, in a small pot, whisk together powdered sugar, milk, vanilla extract and salt. Heat over medium-low heat just until warmed. Brush glaze on top of the doughnuts before serving.

NUTRITION PER SERVING
(1 doughnut)

Calories: 510

Fat: 32g

Sat Fat: 3.5g

Cholesterol: 35mg

Sodium: 410mg

Carbs: 55g

Fiber: 4g

Sugars: 30g

Protein: 5g

Raspberry Jelly-Filled Doughnuts

These doughnuts are a delicious treat that taste like they're straight from the neighborhood doughnut shop. If raspberry isn't your thing, replace the jam with any jam flavor of your choice! (See photo on pages 22–23.)

YIELD
14–16 doughnuts

PREP TIME
20 minutes

TOTAL TIME
1 hour (includes rising time)

1 cup warm skim milk (approximately 100°F)

2 ¼ teaspoons (1 packet) rapid-rise yeast

¼ cup sugar

2 eggs

1 ½ teaspoons vanilla extract

1 teaspoon salt

3 cups gluten-free all-purpose flour

6 tablespoons cold butter, cut into 1-inch cubes

Plastic wrap, for covering dough

Floured parchment paper, for rolling out

Canola oil, for frying

1 cup raspberry jelly

Powdered sugar, for garnish

1 In the bowl of a stand mixer using the paddle attachment, add warm milk and yeast and let stand until it blooms, about 5 minutes.

2 Add sugar, eggs, vanilla extract and salt. Mix until well combined. Slowly add gluten-free all-purpose flour, mixing well as you add the flour.

3 Add butter and mix until dough is totally smooth. Cover with plastic wrap and let rise in a warm area for 30 to 40 minutes until it doubles in size.

4 Turn dough out onto floured parchment paper and roll it out to a ½-inch-thick circle. Cut dough into 14 to 16 circles with a biscuit cutter or the floured rim of a glass.

5 Fill a large, deep pot with approximately 4 inches of canola oil. Heat oil to 350°F. Place doughnuts in hot oil a few at a time, being careful not to overcrowd the pot.

6 Fry each doughnut for approximately 2 minutes per side until it turns golden brown. Drain on a paper towel–lined baking sheet until they are cool enough to handle. Repeat until all doughnuts are fried.

7 Fill a pastry bag fitted with a large round tip with raspberry jelly. Once doughnuts are cool enough to handle, push the tip into each doughnut and gently squeeze the pastry bag to fill. You can also cut a small slit in the side of the doughnut with a knife and fill using a very small spoon if you do not have a pastry bag. Sprinkle doughnuts with powdered sugar before serving.

NUTRITION PER SERVING
(1 doughnut)

Calories: 340

Fat: 23g

Sat Fat: 6g

Cholesterol: 45mg

Sodium: 230mg

Carbs: 47g

Fiber: 3g

Sugars: 27g

Protein: 4g

Strawberry & Mascarpone Cream Danishes

YIELD
12 Danishes

PREP TIME
45 minutes

TOTAL TIME
1 hour
5 minutes

These Danishes are lovely for a weekend brunch or an evening dessert. Fresh strawberries pair beautifully with the mascarpone filling, but if they're not readily available or you like a different fruit better, replace them with blueberries, raspberries or blackberries.

FOR THE CRUST

2 ½ cups gluten-free all-purpose flour

1 cup (2 sticks) chilled butter, cut into cubes

½ teaspoon salt

8 to 12 tablespoons ice water

Plastic wrap, for dough

FOR THE MASCARPONE CREAM FILLING

1 (8 ounce) container mascarpone cheese

2 tablespoons cream cheese

½ cup heavy whipping cream

¼ cup sugar

1 teaspoon vanilla extract

FOR THE TOPPING

1 pound thinly sliced fresh strawberries

1 To make the crust, in a food processor, combine gluten-free all-purpose flour, butter and salt. Pulse a few times until small, pea-sized chunks of butter remain. Add ice water, 1 tablespoon at a time, until dough resembles large curds. Turn dough out onto plastic wrap and form into 1 large disk. Chill for 30 minutes.

2 Preheat oven to 425°F. Once dough is chilled, roll it out and cut into 12 circles. Press dough circles into 12 greased muffin tin cups. Bake crusts for 15 minutes. Remove from oven and set aside.

3 To make the mascarpone cream filling, in the bowl of a stand mixer using the whisk attachment on high speed, whisk together mascarpone cheese, cream cheese, heavy whipping cream, sugar and vanilla extract. Whisk until mixture is creamed together and stiff. Cover and refrigerate until ready to assemble Danishes.

4 To assemble the Danishes, carefully remove crusts from the muffin tin. Spoon approximately 1 ½ to 2 tablespoons of mascarpone cream filling into each crust and then evenly divide sliced strawberries among all the Danishes.

NUTRITION PER SERVING
(1 Danish)

Calories: 430

Fat: 31g

Sat Fat: 18g

Cholesterol: 85mg

Sodium: 270mg

Carbs: 37g

Fiber: 4g

Sugars: 16g

Protein: 5g

Oatmeal Pancakes with Sweet Ricotta & Blueberry Compote

YIELD
6 servings
(2 pancakes
per serving)

PREP TIME
10 minutes

TOTAL TIME
30 minutes

Fluffy and fiber-packed, these oatmeal pancakes taste just like the real deal. Top them with heaping scoops of sweetened ricotta and blueberry compote for a magical Sunday morning meal.

FOR THE SWEET RICOTTA

1 (15 ounce) container part-skim ricotta

3 ½ tablespoons agave nectar

½ teaspoon lemon zest

½ teaspoon vanilla extract

FOR THE BLUEBERRY COMPOTE

1 tablespoon butter

3 cups fresh or frozen blueberries

3 tablespoons agave nectar

3 tablespoons Triple Sec liqueur

½ teaspoon salt

FOR THE PANCAKES

2 cups gluten-free all-purpose flour

1 cup quick cook oats

⅓ cup sugar

1 tablespoon baking powder

1 teaspoon salt

2 eggs

2 cups plus 2 tablespoons milk

Oil, for griddle

1 To make the sweet ricotta topping, in the bowl of a stand mixer using the paddle attachment, beat together part-skim ricotta, agave nectar, lemon zest and vanilla extract until light and fluffy, about 2 minutes. Transfer to a small bowl, cover and refrigerate until ready to serve.

2 To make the blueberry compote, melt butter in a nonstick skillet over medium-high heat. Add blueberries, agave nectar, Triple Sec and salt. Cook, stirring frequently until the liquid around the blueberries becomes thick and syrupy, about 7 to 10 minutes. Remove from heat and set aside until ready to serve.

3 To make the pancakes, in a mixing bowl, whisk together gluten-free all-purpose flour, oats, sugar, baking powder and salt.

4 In a separate bowl, whisk together eggs and milk until light and fluffy. Pour wet ingredients into the dry ingredients and mix until a smooth batter forms.

5 Lightly grease a griddle over medium heat. Pour batter by ¼ cup full onto the griddle and cook approximately 3 to 4 minutes per side. Flip pancakes when bubbles form across the surface of the batter. Repeat until all batter is cooked into pancakes.

6 Serve pancakes topped with sweet ricotta and blueberry compote.

NUTRITION PER SERVING
(2 pancakes)

Calories: 870

Fat: 50g

Sat Fat: 12g

Cholesterol: 105mg

Sodium: 1,040mg

Carbs: 88g

Fiber: 7g

Sugars: 42g

Protein: 21g

YIELD
4 servings
(2 pancakes
per serving)

PREP TIME
10 minutes

TOTAL TIME
25 minutes

Buckwheat Pancakes with Strawberry Compote & Honey Butter

Made with naturally gluten-free flours, these pancakes pack a nutritious punch, but still have that familiar buttermilk flavor. Topped with sweet strawberries, these pancakes will become a weekend family favorite.

FOR THE STRAWBERRY COMPOTE

3 cups thinly sliced strawberries

¼ cup sugar

Zest of 1 lemon

1 teaspoon lemon juice

FOR THE HONEY BUTTER

½ cup (1 stick) butter, softened

2 tablespoons honey

FOR THE PANCAKES

1 cup buckwheat flour

½ cup coconut flour

2 tablespoons sugar

2 teaspoons baking powder

½ teaspoon salt

1 cup buttermilk

1 cup skim milk

2 eggs

2 tablespoons coconut oil

Nonstick cooking spray, for greasing pan

1 To make the strawberry compote, in a small saucepan, combine strawberries, sugar, lemon zest and lemon juice. Heat over medium heat, stirring frequently, until a thick syrupy sauce forms around the strawberries, about 7 to 10 minutes. Remove from heat and set aside until ready to serve.

2 To make the honey butter, mix together butter and honey. Set aside until ready to serve.

3 To make the pancakes, in a mixing bowl, whisk together buckwheat flour, coconut flour, sugar, baking powder and salt.

4 In a separate bowl, whisk together buttermilk, skim milk, eggs and coconut oil. Pour wet ingredients into the dry ingredients and mix until a smooth batter forms.

5 Preheat a griddle pan or a large skillet over medium heat. Spray pan lightly with nonstick cooking spray. Ladle batter into the pan, using approximately ¼ cup of batter per pancake. Cook each pancake until golden brown on the bottom side and small bubbles begin forming on the surface of the batter. Flip each pancake and cook an additional 2 minutes. Repeat until all batter is cooked into pancakes.

6 Serve pancakes topped with strawberry compote and honey butter.

NUTRITION PER SERVING
(2 pancakes)

Calories: 670

Fat: 38g

Sat Fat: 25g

Cholesterol: 180mg

Sodium: 430mg

Carbs: 74g

Fiber: 11g

Sugars: 40g

Protein: 14g

Belgian-Style Waffles

Large, fluffy and filled with good-for-you grains, these waffles are a wonderful substitute for traditional Belgian waffles. They're sweetened with just a small amount of sugar and enhanced with the flavor of vanilla soymilk.

YIELD
4 waffles

PREP TIME
10 minutes

TOTAL TIME
20 minutes

1 ½ cups buckwheat flour

¼ cup coconut flour

¼ cup teff flour

2 tablespoons sugar

2 teaspoons baking powder

½ teaspoon salt

2 ½ cups vanilla soymilk

1 tablespoon lemon juice

1 egg yolk

2 tablespoons canola or vegetable oil

2 teaspoons vanilla extract

3 egg whites

Nonstick cooking spray, for greasing waffle iron

1 In a mixing bowl, whisk together buckwheat flour, coconut flour, teff flour, sugar, baking powder and salt.

2 In a separate bowl, whisk together vanilla soymilk, lemon juice, egg yolk, canola or vegetable oil and vanilla extract. Slowly mix dry ingredients into the wet ingredients.

3 Using a handheld mixer, beat egg whites until stiff peaks form. Fold egg whites into the batter.

4 Preheat waffle iron according to manufacturer's instructions. Lightly grease waffle iron with nonstick cooking spray. Fill the waffle iron about ⅔ full and cook until golden brown on both sides. Repeat until all batter is cooked into waffles.

NUTRITION PER SERVING
(1 waffle)

Calories: 250

Fat: 6g

Sat Fat: 1.5g

Cholesterol: 30mg

Sodium: 460mg

Carbs: 40g

Fiber: 6g

Sugars: 9g

Protein: 10g

Orange Cinnamon Rolls with Orange Glaze

Soft and gooey, like a traditional cinnamon bun, but packed with luscious hints of orange, these rolls are sure to impress! If you like a crunchy bun, toss a handful of crushed walnuts into the filling.

FOR THE DOUGH

2 ½ cups gluten-free all-purpose flour

¼ cup sugar

2 ¼ teaspoons (1 packet) rapid-rise yeast

1 teaspoon salt

6 tablespoons butter, softened

1 cup warm milk

1 egg

1 ½ teaspoons vanilla extract

Greased parchment paper or silicon mat

2 tablespoons butter, melted

FOR THE FILLING

1 cup sugar

2 teaspoons orange zest

1 tablespoon ground cinnamon

FOR THE ORANGE GLAZE

2 cups powdered sugar

6 tablespoons cream cheese, softened

2 tablespoons milk

1 tablespoon freshly squeezed orange juice

1 teaspoon orange zest

1 To make the dough, in the bowl of a stand mixer using the paddle attachment, beat together gluten-free all-purpose flour, sugar, yeast and salt.

2 Add butter and mix until coarse crumbs form. Slowly drizzle in warm milk while mixing on low speed. Add egg and vanilla extract and mix to combine.

3 Cover and place in a warm area to rise for 1 hour or until dough has doubled in size.

4 To make the filling, in a small bowl, mix together sugar and orange zest with fingers until lightly colored and fragrant. Add cinnamon and mix to combine.

5 Press dough into a large (8 x 16-inch) rectangle on a greased sheet of parchment paper.

6 Brush melted butter over surface of the dough. Sprinkle filling over the dough evenly, leaving a 1-inch border around the dough.

7 With long edge of the dough toward you, gently roll dough forward with the parchment paper. The dough should release from the paper as you roll. Cut rolled dough into 12 slices using a sharp knife.

8 Place each roll of dough into a greased muffin tin cup. Let rolls rise for another hour until puffy.

9 Preheat oven to 350°F. Place rolls on a baking sheet lined with a silicon mat or greased parchment paper. Bake for 20 to 25 minutes until golden brown.

10 To make the orange glaze, in the bowl of a stand mixer using the paddle attachment, combine powdered sugar, cream cheese, milk, orange juice and orange zest. Beat until smooth and runny. Add additional milk to reach desired consistency. Drizzle glaze over rolls once they are completely cooled.

YIELD
8 biscuits

PREP TIME
15 minutes

TOTAL TIME
1 hour
5 minutes

Buttermilk Cheddar Breakfast Biscuits

A Southern classic, these biscuits are best served topped with a hearty gravy or alongside a beef stew.

Parchment paper, for lining baking sheet

2 cups gluten-free all-purpose flour

1 cup grated sharp cheddar cheese

2 teaspoons baking powder

1 teaspoon salt

8 tablespoons (1 stick) very cold butter

¾ cup buttermilk

1 Line a baking sheet with parchment paper and set aside.

2 In a mixing bowl, whisk together gluten-free all-purpose flour, cheddar cheese, baking powder and salt. Cut in butter until pea-sized crumbles form.

3 Add buttermilk and mix until dough pulls together.

4 Transfer dough to a clean surface and roll out into a large rectangle that is approximately 1 inch thick. Using a biscuit cutter, cut out 8 equal-sized biscuits and place them on the prepared baking sheet.

5 Cover biscuits and place in freezer for 30 minutes.

6 Preheat oven to 450°F. Bake for 18 to 20 minutes until lightly golden.

NUTRITION PER SERVING
(2 biscuits)

Calories: 550

Fat: 35g

Sat Fat: 20g

Cholesterol: 95mg

Sodium: 1,430mg

Carbs: 49g

Fiber: 6g

Sugars: 4g

Protein: 15g

YIELD
10 slices

PREP TIME
10 minutes

TOTAL TIME
2 hours
(includes
rising time)

White Sandwich Bread

Always keep a loaf of this sandwich bread in the freezer. It comes in handy when you need lunch on the run or a piece of toast to go with your scrambled eggs. If you make the loaf ahead of time, freeze individual slices to use one at a time, as desired.

Nonstick cooking spray, for greasing loaf pan

2 cups brown rice flour

1 cup white rice flour

1 cup potato starch

2½ teaspoons xanthan gum

1 teaspoon baking powder

1 teaspoon kosher salt

2¼ teaspoons (1 packet) rapid-rise yeast

2 cups warm water

1 teaspoon honey

2 eggs

2 tablespoons olive oil

Oiled plastic wrap, for covering dough

1 Lightly spray a 9 x 5-inch loaf pan with nonstick cooking spray and set aside.

2 In the bowl of a stand mixer using the paddle attachment, combine brown rice flour, white rice flour, potato starch, xanthan gum, baking powder and kosher salt.

3 In a separate bowl, combine yeast, warm water and honey. Gently whisk and let sit for 5 minutes until yeast blooms.

4 Add eggs and olive oil to the yeast and water mixture and gently whisk to combine. Pour wet mixture into the dry flour mixture and mix on medium speed until combined and very sticky.

5 Pour batter into prepared loaf pan and cover with oiled plastic wrap. Let rise in a warm place for about 1 hour until dough reaches the top of the pan.

6 Preheat oven to 350°F. Remove plastic wrap and bake for 1 hour until bread sounds hollow when tapped.

7 Let bread cool in pan for 5 minutes, then remove and cool on a wire rack.

NUTRITION PER SERVING
(1 slice)

Calories: 240

Fat: 5g

Sat Fat: 1g

Cholesterol: 105mg

Sodium: 230mg

Carbs: 45g

Fiber: 2g

Sugars: 1g

Protein: 4g

YIELD
10 slices

PREP TIME
45 minutes

TOTAL TIME
1 hour
25 minutes
(includes
rising time)

**NUTRITION
PER SERVING**
(1 slice)

Calories: 190

Fat: 8g

Sat Fat: 1g

Cholesterol:
105mg

Sodium:
310mg

Carbs: 29g

Fiber: 2g

Sugars: 3g

Protein: 4g

Multigrain Sandwich Bread

If sandwiches are a big deal in your household, make several loaves of this bread at a time and freeze them to use all week. Whether you want a peanut butter and jelly or a BLT, this bread is just the way to hold it together. If you make the loaf ahead of time, freeze individual slices to use one at a time, as desired.

Nonstick cooking spray,
for greasing loaf pan

1¼ cups warm water

2 tablespoons honey

2¼ teaspoons (1 packet)
rapid-rise yeast

1 cup potato starch

⅔ cup sorghum flour

¾ cup millet flour

⅓ cup ground flax seed meal

2 teaspoons xanthan gum

1½ teaspoons sea salt

2 eggs, beaten

¼ cup olive oil

Oiled plastic wrap,
for covering dough

1 Lightly spray a 9 x 5-inch loaf pan with nonstick cooking spray and set aside.

2 In a mixing bowl, gently mix together warm water, honey and yeast. Let sit for about 5 minutes until yeast blooms.

3 In the bowl of a stand mixer using the paddle attachment, mix together potato starch, sorghum flour, millet flour, flax seed meal, xanthan gum and sea salt.

4 Add yeast mixture to the dry ingredients and mix to incorporate. Add eggs and olive oil and mix until the batter has come together.

5 Transfer batter to prepared loaf pan and cover with oiled plastic wrap. Let rise in a warm place until dough reaches the top of the pan, about 30 minutes.

6 Preheat oven to 350°F. Remove plastic wrap and bake for 30 to 40 minutes until bread sounds hollow when tapped.

7 Let bread cool in pan for 5 minutes, then remove and cool on a wire rack.

FAN FAVORITE

YIELD
8 rolls

PREP TIME
20 minutes

TOTAL TIME
2 hours
(includes
rising time)

Brioche Rolls

Craving a taste of Paris? These brioche rolls will take your taste buds on a trip to France. They're super-soft with just a hint of sweetness.

Nonstick cooking spray, for greasing cake pan

1½ cups gluten-free all-purpose flour

3 tablespoons sugar

2¼ teaspoons (1 package) rapid-rise yeast

¼ teaspoon sea salt

½ cup warm milk

2 eggs, room temperature

½ teaspoon apple cider vinegar

6 tablespoons butter, softened

Oiled plastic wrap, for covering dough

1 Preheat oven to 375°F. Lightly grease a round cake pan with nonstick cooking spray and set aside.

2 In the bowl of a stand mixer using the paddle attachment, mix together gluten-free all-purpose flour, sugar, yeast and sea salt.

3 Add warm milk, eggs and apple cider vinegar to the dry ingredients and mix until well combined.

4 Add butter 1 tablespoon at a time, ensuring that each piece is fully incorporated before adding the next. Dough will be soft and sticky.

5 Scoop dough into prepared cake pan using an ice cream scoop or a large spoon to shape into rolls. Smooth the tops with wet hands. Cover with oiled plastic wrap and let rise in a warm place for 30 minutes until rolls are slightly puffed.

6 Remove plastic wrap. Bake for 20 minutes at 375°F, then bake for another 20 minutes at 325°F or until golden on top and rolls bounce back when touched.

NUTRITION PER SERVING
(1 roll)

Calories: 185

Fat: 9.6g

Sat Fat: 6g

Cholesterol: 70mg

Sodium: 99mg

Carbs: 20.5g

Fiber: 0.4g

Sugars: 5.5g

Protein: 2.6g

YIELD
6 biscuits

PREP TIME
15 minutes

TOTAL TIME
1 hour
15 minutes
(includes
chilling time)

**NUTRITION
PER SERVING**
(1 biscuit)

Calories: 560

Fat: 36g

Sat Fat: 21g

Cholesterol:
190mg

Sodium:
900mg

Carbs: 54g

Fiber: 7g

Sugars: 4g

Protein: 11g

Flaky Home-Style Biscuits

These biscuits are great for breakfast, lunch or dinner. They make a great accompaniment to comfort food dishes or are terrific with jam and a cup of coffee.

Parchment paper, for lining baking sheet

3 ½ cups gluten-free all-purpose flour, plus additional for rolling out

2 teaspoons baking powder

1 teaspoon salt

1 cup (2 sticks) cold butter, cut into cubes

3 eggs

⅔ cup buttermilk

1 Preheat oven to 400°F. Line a baking sheet with parchment paper and set aside.

2 In a large bowl, combine gluten-free all-purpose flour, baking powder and salt. Add butter and cut in with a fork until crumbly and pea-sized chunks remain.

3 Add eggs and buttermilk and mix to combine with a fork. The dough will be slightly sticky.

4 Turn dough out onto a floured countertop and roll the dough out to a 1-inch-thick rectangle. Fold dough into thirds lengthwise, then fold into thirds widthwise.

5 Roll out dough to ½-inch thickness and repeat the folding and rolling process twice more.

6 Roll dough into a very thick square. Cut out biscuits into 6 squares using a pizza cutter or into circles using a biscuit cutter. Place biscuits in freezer for 20 to 30 minutes to chill.

7 Place biscuits on prepared baking sheet and bake for 15 to 20 minutes until golden brown.

Caramelized Onion Focaccia

This flat, baked Italian bread is soft on the inside with a thin crispy crust. Caramelized onions bring a strong flavor to the topping.

YIELD
8 slices

PREP TIME
25 minutes

TOTAL TIME
1 hour
30 minutes
(includes
rising time)

FOR THE FOCACCIA

3 cups gluten-free
all-purpose flour

2 teaspoons salt

2 cups warm water

2 ¼ teaspoons (1 packet)
rapid-rise yeast

2 tablespoons olive oil plus
additional for oiling the
baking sheet

Plastic wrap, for covering dough

FOR THE CARAMELIZED ONIONS

2 tablespoons butter

4 cups thinly sliced red onions

1 tablespoon sugar

1 teaspoon sea salt plus extra
for garnish

1 Preheat oven to 450°F. Prepare a baking sheet by rubbing it generously with olive oil and set aside.

2 To make the focaccia, in the bowl of a stand mixer using a paddle attachment, combine gluten-free all-purpose flour and salt.

3 In a separate bowl, whisk together warm water and yeast. Let sit for 5 minutes until foamy. Whisk in olive oil and then pour wet ingredients into the mixer with the dry ingredients and mix on low speed just until combined. Cover bowl with plastic wrap and let dough rise for 1 hour.

4 To make the caramelized onions, melt butter in a large nonstick pan over medium heat. Add red onions, sugar and sea salt and cook, stirring occasionally, until onions are browned and caramelized, about 25 to 30 minutes.

5 Rub hands with olive oil and then press the dough out onto prepared baking sheet. Gently pierce dough with your fingers and then sprinkle the caramelized onions evenly on top of the dough. Sprinkle sea salt on top of the dough and bake for 20 to 25 minutes until lightly golden.

NUTRITION PER SERVING
(1 slice)

Calories: 260

Fat: 8g

Sat Fat: 2.5g

Cholesterol:
10mg

Sodium:
910mg

Carbs: 46g

Fiber: 6g

Sugars: 8g

Protein: 6g

PREP TIME
20 minutes

TOTAL TIME
2 hours
30 minutes
(includes
rising time)

NUTRITION
PER SERVING
(1 bun)

Calories: 330

Fat: 13g

Sat Fat: 2g

Cholesterol:
70mg

Sodium:
950mg

Carbs: 50g

Fiber: 5g

Sugars: 13g

Protein: 8g

Hamburger Buns

With these hamburger buns, you will never have to have a bunless burger again! These buns are soft and sturdy, making them perfect for those summertime backyard barbecues. Make plenty so you can bring them to an impromptu BBQ gathering. If you make the buns ahead of time, wrap each bun in foil to freeze and then use one at a time as desired.

Parchment paper and
nonstick cooking spray,
for lining and greasing
baking sheet

2 ¼ teaspoons (1 packet)
rapid-rise yeast

¾ cup warm water

2 ½ cups gluten-free
all-purpose flour

2 teaspoons salt

1 ½ teaspoons
baking powder

2 eggs, room temperature

⅓ cup sugar

¼ cup vegetable oil

½ teaspoon apple
cider vinegar

Oiled plastic wrap, for
covering dough

1 egg white

Sesame seeds, for garnish
(optional)

1 Line a baking sheet with parchment paper and lightly grease with nonstick cooking spray and set aside.

2 In a mixing bowl, combine yeast and warm water and let sit until puffy, about 5 minutes.

3 In a separate bowl, whisk together gluten-free all-purpose flour, salt and baking powder.

4 In the bowl of a stand mixer using the paddle attachment, combine eggs, sugar, vegetable oil and apple cider vinegar and beat at medium speed until well combined.

5 Gradually add dry ingredients into the wet ingredients, mixing well after each addition. Mix until fully incorporated. Add yeast and water mixture and mix well. The dough will be sticky.

6 Divide dough into 6 equal portions and, using wet hands, shape into buns and place them on prepared baking sheet. Cover with oiled plastic wrap and let rise in a warm place for 1 hour or until doubled in size.

7 Preheat oven to 375°F. Remove plastic wrap from the buns and lightly brush them with egg white, being careful not to collapse them. Sprinkle with sesame seeds, if desired.

8 Bake buns for 15 minutes. Reduce temperature to 350°F and cover buns with a sheet of parchment paper and bake for another 5 to 10 minutes, until buns are fully cooked inside or a thermometer inserted into the center reads 200°F.

9 Let buns cool on a cooling rack. Split buns with a knife once they are completely cool.

⊗ No-Rise Pizza Crust

YIELD
4 individual
pizza crusts

PREP TIME
5 minutes

TOTAL TIME
20 minutes

A no-fuss recipe for nights when you want a pizza pronto! Add your favorite toppings to this crust and you'll have dinner ready in no time!

1 cup warm water

2 ¼ teaspoons (1 packet) rapid-rise yeast

1 tablespoon olive oil

1 tablespoon sugar

2 ¾ cups gluten-free all-purpose flour

¼ cup grated Parmesan cheese

½ teaspoon sea salt

Floured parchment paper, for rolling out

1 Preheat oven to 450°F. In the bowl of a stand mixer using the paddle attachment combine warm water, yeast, olive oil and sugar and let sit until yeast is puffy, about 5 minutes.

2 In a large bowl, whisk together gluten-free all-purpose flour, Parmesan cheese and sea salt .

3 Add half of flour mixture to yeast and water mixture and beat on low until well incorporated. Add remaining flour mixture and mix until dough is thoroughly combined.

4 Turn dough out onto a floured sheet of parchment paper and divide into 4 equal-sized balls. Oil hands and gently roll balls into disks. Roll out using another floured piece of parchment paper on top of the dough. Roll into rustic-shaped pizzas that are approximately ½ inch thick.

5 Top as desired and bake for 10 to 15 minutes.

NUTRITION PER SERVING
(1 crust)

Calories: 350

Fat: 8g

Sat Fat: 1.5g

Cholesterol: 5mg

Sodium: 420mg

Carbs: 64g

Fiber: 9g

Sugars: 6g

Protein: 12g

YIELD
4 individual pizzas

PREP TIME
15 minutes

TOTAL TIME
30 minutes

Margherita Pizza

Just like the classic recipe, this No-Rise Pizza Crust is topped with fresh mozzarella, cherry tomatoes and fresh basil. For a flavor twist, drizzle the pizza with balsamic vinegar just before serving.

Parchment paper, for lining baking sheets

1 recipe No-Rise Pizza Crust dough (page 66)

1 cup marinara sauce, divided

24 small fresh mozzarella balls, divided

2 cups cherry tomatoes, halved and divided

¼ cup olive oil

½ cup thinly sliced basil strips

1 Preheat oven to 450°F. Line 2 baking sheets with parchment paper and set aside.

2 Make No-Rise Pizza Crust dough and roll out as directed into 4 rustic-shaped pizzas. Spread each pizza crust dough with ¼ cup marinara sauce, leaving room on the edges for a crust.

3 Add 6 mozzarella balls and ½ cup cherry tomatoes to each pizza. Drizzle each pizza with 1 tablespoon olive oil.

4 Bake for 10 to 15 minutes until golden and cheese is bubbly. Top with fresh basil strips before serving.

NUTRITION PER SERVING
(1 pizza)

Calories: 790

Fat: 37g

Sat Fat: 8g

Cholesterol: 5mg

Sodium: 1,420mg

Carbs: 97g

Fiber: 11g

Sugars: 36g

Protein: 26g

Pesto, Artichoke & Sweet Sausage Pizza

Pesto, artichokes and sweet sausage blend together on top of this easy-to-make, no-rise pizza. If you like your pizza to give you a kick, top this with red pepper flakes.

YIELD
4 individual pizzas

PREP TIME
15 minutes

TOTAL TIME
30 minutes

Parchment paper, for lining baking sheets

1 recipe No-Rise Pizza Crust dough (page 66)

1 tablespoon olive oil

1 pound sweet Italian sausage, casings removed

1 (7 ounce) container pesto sauce

1 cup chopped artichoke hearts

2 cups grated mozzarella cheese

1 cup grated Parmesan cheese

1 Preheat oven to 450°F. Line 2 baking sheets with parchment paper and set aside.

2 Make No-Rise Pizza Crust dough and roll out as directed into 4 rustic-shaped pizzas.

3 In a skillet, heat olive oil over medium-high heat. Add sweet Italian sausage and, using a wooden spoon, break sausage into small pieces. Cook, stirring occasionally until sausage is browned, about 7 minutes. Remove from heat and set aside.

4 Spread each pizza crust dough evenly with pesto sauce, leaving room on the edges for a crust.

5 Divide cooked and crumbled sausage and artichokes evenly among the 4 pizzas. Top each with mozzarella cheese and Parmesan cheese.

6 Bake for 10 to 15 minutes until golden and cheese is bubbly.

NUTRITION PER SERVING
(1 pizza)

Calories: 1,070

Fat: 63g

Sat Fat: 22g

Cholesterol: 110mg

Sodium: 3,170mg

Carbs: 75g

Fiber: 11g

Sugars: 7g

Protein: 60g

⭐ # Thin-Crust Pizza

YIELD
1 (9 x 13-inch)
pizza
(4 servings)

PREP TIME
20 minutes

TOTAL TIME
1 hour
30 minutes
(includes
rising time)

This thin-crust pizza tastes just like a pizza served up in Tuscany, Italy. It's thin, crispy and bakes in just 15 minutes.

¾ cup warm water

2 ¼ teaspoons (1 packet) rapid-rise yeast

1 tablespoon olive oil, plus olive oil for greasing bowl

1 tablespoon sugar

1 ¼ cups gluten-free all-purpose flour

1 teaspoon sea salt

1 tablespoon apple cider vinegar

Parchment paper, for lining baking sheets

Oiled plastic wrap, for covering dough

Additional ⅛ cup gluten-free all-purpose flour for rolling out

1 In the bowl of a stand mixer using the paddle attachment, combine warm water, yeast, olive oil and sugar and let sit until yeast is puffy, about 5 minutes.

2 In a large bowl, whisk together gluten-free all-purpose flour and sea salt.

3 Add half of flour mixture to yeast and water mixture and beat on low until well incorporated. Add remaining flour mixture and apple cider vinegar and mix until dough is very sticky and smooth.

4 Place dough in an oiled bowl and cover with oiled plastic wrap. Let rise in a warm place for 1 hour.

5 Preheat oven to 450°F. Turn dough out onto a parchment-lined baking sheet and sprinkle gluten-free all-purpose flour on top of the dough. Gently stretch and press dough into the baking sheet with your hands.

6 Top as desired and bake for 15 to 20 minutes.

NUTRITION PER SERVING
(2 slices)

Calories: 210

Fat: 5g

Sat Fat: 0.5g

Cholesterol: 0mg

Sodium: 610mg

Carbs: 36g

Fiber: 7g

Sugars: 4g

Protein: 8g

Pepperoni & Mushroom Pizza

A pizzeria classic simply topped with pepperoni and mushrooms. For a more intense flavor, add chopped garlic to the mushrooms as you sauté them.

1 recipe Thin-Crust Pizza dough (page 70)

2 tablespoons olive oil

2 cups thinly sliced mushrooms

1 cup pizza sauce

3 cups shredded mozzarella cheese

1 ½ cups sliced pepperoni

1 Preheat oven to 450°F. Make Thin-Crust Pizza dough, press into baking sheet and let rise as directed.

2 In a large skillet, heat olive oil over medium-high heat and sauté mushrooms until browned, about 5 to 7 minutes. Let cool and set aside.

3 Spread pizza sauce on top of dough, leaving room on the edges for a crust.

4 Sprinkle mozzarella cheese on top of the sauce and add mushrooms and pepperoni to the pizza.

5 Bake for 15 to 20 minutes until golden and cheese is bubbly.

 FAN FAVORITE

YIELD
1 (9 x 13-inch) pizza
(4 servings)

PREP TIME
15 minutes

TOTAL TIME
30 minutes

NUTRITION PER SERVING
(2 slices)

Calories: 610

Fat: 33g

Sat Fat: 15g

Cholesterol: 65mg

Sodium: 1,650mg

Carbs: 47g

Fiber: 8g

Sugars: 7g

Protein: 33g

YIELD
1 (9 x 13-inch)
pizza
(4 servings)

PREP TIME
15 minutes

TOTAL TIME
30 minutes

Green Garden Pizza

Garden-fresh green vegetables top this white pizza. If green isn't your thing, pick any veggies to complement the lightly flavored cheese.

NUTRITION PER SERVING
(2 slices)

Calories: 630

Fat: 32g

Sat Fat: 18g

Cholesterol: 90mg

Sodium: 2,350mg

Carbs: 47g

Fiber: 8g

Sugars: 6g

Protein: 44g

1 recipe Thin-Crust Pizza dough (page 70)

1 cup ricotta cheese

2 cups grated mozzarella cheese

1 teaspoon garlic powder

1 teaspoon sea salt

1 cup chopped artichoke hearts

1 cup chopped spinach

1 cup chopped broccoli florets

1 cup grated Parmesan cheese

1 Preheat oven to 450°F. Make Thin Crust Pizza dough, press into baking sheet and let rise as directed.

2 Spread ricotta cheese evenly across surface of dough, leaving room on the edges for a crust. Sprinkle mozzarella cheese on top of the ricotta and then sprinkle with garlic powder and sea salt.

3 Distribute artichoke hearts, spinach and broccoli florets evenly across surface of the pizza and top with Parmesan cheese.

4 Bake for 15 to 20 minutes until golden and cheese is bubbly.

Stuffed-Crust Pizza

Miss that restaurant-style, stuffed-crust pizza? Miss no more with this easy-to-make recipe that uses string cheese as a filler.

1 cup warm water

1 tablespoon olive oil plus olive oil, for greasing bowl

1 tablespoon sugar

2 ¼ teaspoons (1 packet) rapid-rise yeast

1 ½ cups gluten-free all-purpose flour

1 teaspoon sea salt

1 tablespoon apple cider vinegar

Parchment paper, for lining cake pan

Oiled plastic wrap, for covering dough

Additional ⅛ cup gluten-free all-purpose flour for rolling out

2 string mozzarella cheese sticks, sliced in half lengthwise

1 In the bowl of a stand mixer using the paddle attachment, combine warm water, olive oil, sugar and yeast and let sit until yeast is puffy, about 5 minutes.

2 In a large bowl, whisk together gluten-free all-purpose flour and sea salt.

3 Add half of flour mixture to yeast and water mixture and beat on low until well incorporated. Add remaining flour mixture and apple cider vinegar and mix until dough is very sticky and smooth.

4 Place dough in an oiled bowl and cover with oiled plastic wrap. Let rise in a warm place for 1 hour.

5 Cut out a parchment circle and place it on the bottom of a 9-inch round cake pan.

6 Preheat oven to 450°F. Turn dough out onto prepared cake pan and sprinkle gluten-free all-purpose flour on top of the dough. Gently stretch and press the dough into the cake pan with your hands, forming a very large "dough wall" around the edges and a well in the middle.

7 Place mozzarella cheese sticks around inner edges of the dough wall and gently press toward the edge of the cake pan. With wet hands, gently fold dough over mozzarella sticks. You should have a pizza with a sunken center circle and a large ring of dough around the edges.

8 Let rise an additional 30 minutes. Top as desired and bake for 25 to 30 minutes.

 FAN FAVORITE

YIELD
1 deep-dish, 9-inch pizza (4 servings)

PREP TIME
15 minutes

TOTAL TIME
1 hour 30 minutes (includes rising time)

NUTRITION PER SERVING
(2 slices)

Calories: 300

Fat: 9g

Sat Fat: 1.5g

Cholesterol: 5mg

Sodium: 710mg

Carbs: 52g

Fiber: 7g

Sugars: 5g

Protein: 9g

Veggie Pizza

YIELD
1 deep-dish,
9-inch pizza
(4 servings)

PREP TIME
15 minutes

TOTAL TIME
45 minutes

Basic veggies top this stuffed-crust pizza. If you're a meat lover, add pepperoni, sausage or salami.

1 recipe Stuffed-Crust Pizza dough (page 73)

Pinch of salt

Water, for boiling

¼ cup small broccoli florets, blanched

Ice water

½ cup marinara sauce

¼ cup thinly sliced red bell pepper

¼ small sweet yellow onion, thinly sliced

¼ cup shredded mozzarella cheese

2 tablespoons olive oil

1 Preheat oven to 450°F. Make Stuffed-Crust Pizza dough and let rise as directed.

2 Bring a large pot of salted water to boil and add broccoli florets. Boil for 3 to 5 minutes until just tender, then remove and plunge them into a bowl of ice water. Remove broccoli florets and set them aside to dry.

3 Spread marinara sauce evenly across the stuffed-crust dough. Add broccoli florets, red bell pepper and onions.

4 Sprinkle mozzarella cheese over the vegetables. Brush exposed crust with olive oil.

5 Bake for 25 to 30 minutes until golden and cheese is bubbly.

NUTRITION PER SERVING
(2 slices)

Calories: 400

Fat: 18g

Sat Fat: 4g

Cholesterol: 10mg

Sodium: 880mg

Carbs: 56g

Fiber: 8g

Sugars: 8g

Protein: 12g

Prosciutto & Pineapple Pizza

Italy meets Hawaii in this stuffed-crust sweet and salty pizza.

YIELD
1 deep-dish,
9-inch pizza
(4 servings)

PREP TIME
15 minutes

TOTAL TIME
45 minutes

1 recipe Stuffed-Crust Pizza dough (page 73)

½ cup pizza sauce

2 cups grated provolone cheese

1 cup grated mozzarella cheese

1 cup sliced prosciutto

1 cup chopped pineapple

2 tablespoons olive oil

1 Preheat oven to 450°F. Make Stuffed-Crust Pizza dough and let rise as directed.

2 Spread pizza sauce evenly across the stuffed-crust dough. Sprinkle provolone and mozzarella cheese on top of the pizza sauce and then top with prosciutto and pineapple.

3 Brush exposed crust with olive oil.

4 Bake for 25 to 30 minutes until golden and cheese is bubbly.

NUTRITION PER SERVING
(2 slices)

Calories: 660

Fat: 33g

Sat Fat: 14g

Cholesterol: 65mg

Sodium: 1,620mg

Carbs: 66g

Fiber: 8g

Sugars: 15g

Protein: 32g

CHAPTER THREE

Soups
& Salads

3

Garden Fresh Minestrone Soup

YIELD
8 servings

PREP TIME
15 minutes

TOTAL TIME
30 minutes

Get a healthy dose of your essential vitamins and minerals from this Italian soup that is chock-full of good-for-you vegetables and lean protein. The ingredients in this soup are easy to substitute, depending on your preference or what's in season. So get creative and play with your food!

2 tablespoons olive oil

1 cup diced sweet yellow onion

2 cloves garlic, minced

8 cups (64 ounces) vegetable stock

2 ½ cups butternut squash, peeled and cubed

2 ½ cups russet potatoes, peeled and cubed

1 cup diced carrots

1 cup diced tomatoes

2 teaspoons salt

1 teaspoon oregano

6 cups chopped kale or spinach

1 cup gluten-free brown rice elbow pasta

1 (16 ounce) can cannellini beans, rinsed and drained

Chopped parsley, for garnish

Grated Parmesan cheese, for garnish

1 In a large pot, heat olive oil over medium-high heat. Add onions and cook, stirring occasionally, until the onions are translucent, about 5 minutes. Add garlic and cook 1 additional minute.

2 Add vegetable stock, butternut squash, potatoes, carrots, tomatoes, salt and oregano and bring to a boil. Reduce heat to medium-low, cover and simmer for 5 minutes.

3 Add kale or spinach, brown rice pasta and cannellini beans, cover and cook an additional 10 minutes until all of the vegetables and pasta are soft.

4 Ladle soup into bowls and garnish with parsley and grated Parmesan cheese, if desired. Serve immediately.

NUTRITION PER SERVING

Calories: 510

Fat: 11g

Sat Fat: 2g

Cholesterol: 10mg

Sodium: 1,780mg

Carbs: 85g

Fiber: 13g

Sugars: 12g

Protein: 21g

Red Curry Seafood Stew

This Thai-inspired soup made with spicy red curry paste is tempered by cooling coconut milk and tangy lime juice. The play of spicy, tangy and sweet highlights the seafood medley of scallops and shrimp alongside a variety of veggies. The scallops have a fleshy texture, a mildly sweet flavor and are full of vitamin B_{12}.

YIELD
6 servings

PREP TIME
15 minutes

TOTAL TIME
30 minutes

2 tablespoons Thai red curry paste

2 (14 ounce) cans coconut milk, divided

2 cups chicken or fish stock

3 tablespoons fish sauce

2 tablespoons brown sugar

¼ cup rice vinegar

¼ cup lime juice

3 cups snow peas

2 cups chopped bok choy

2 cups sliced mushrooms

1 red bell pepper, julienne cut (thin strips)

¼ cup chopped cilantro leaves (plus extra for garnish)

1 pound bay scallops

1 pound shrimp, peeled and deveined

Salt, to taste

1 In a large pot over medium heat, combine curry paste and 1 can of coconut milk. Stir to dissolve curry paste.

2 Add remaining can of coconut milk, along with chicken or fish stock, fish sauce, brown sugar, rice vinegar and lime juice. Bring to a boil and cook for about 2 minutes.

3 Lower heat to a simmer and add snow peas, bok choy, mushrooms, red pepper and cilantro. Cook for 6 to 8 minutes, or until vegetables are tender but still crisp.

4 Add bay scallops and shrimp and cook for 5 minutes. Taste and season with salt, if desired. Serve immediately in bowls and garnish with chopped cilantro.

NUTRITION PER SERVING

Calories: 490

Fat: 29g

Sat Fat: 23g

Cholesterol: 125mg

Sodium: 1,980mg

Carbs: 31g

Fiber: 2g

Sugars: 12g

Protein: 25g

YIELD
4 to 6 servings

PREP TIME
10 minutes

TOTAL TIME
40 minutes

French Onion Soup

Partake in gooey, bubbly, cheesy Gruyère goodness with this traditional recipe for French onion soup. A dash of white wine amplifies the aroma of caramelized onions that play against the earthiness of thyme, bay leaf and parsley. This soup can be made vegetarian easily by substituting vegetable broth for the beef broth. For the bread, use the White Sandwich Bread on page 59.

5 tablespoons butter or margarine

3 medium-sized Vidalia or sweet yellow onions, cut in half and then sliced into very thin half-moon slivers

3 medium-sized red onions, cut in half and then sliced into very thin half-moon slivers

2 tablespoons sugar

1 teaspoon salt

2 cups dry white wine

1 teaspoon cornstarch

6 cups beef broth

1 teaspoon dried thyme

1 bay leaf

1 tablespoon dried parsley

Salt, to taste

6 slices gluten-free bread, cut into large circles

1 pound grated block Gruyère cheese

1 In a large pot, heat butter over medium-high heat. Add yellow and red onions, sugar and salt and cook, stirring occasionally, until onions are caramelized and browned, about 12 to 15 minutes.

2 Add dry white wine and cook until the wine has fully reduced to a thick, syrupy consistency.

3 Stir cornstarch into the beef broth and pour mixture into the pot. Add thyme, bay leaf and parsley. Reduce heat to medium-low, cover and simmer for 15 to 20 minutes.

4 Taste soup and adjust seasoning as needed. Preheat oven on broil setting.

5 Ladle soup into 4 to 6 ovenproof bowls. Place a round slice of gluten-free bread on top of each bowl of soup. Top with a generous portion of grated Gruyère cheese.

6 Broil each bowl of soup until cheese is golden and bubbly, about 1 to 2 minutes. Serve immediately.

NUTRITION PER SERVING

Calories: 930

Fat: 53g

Sat Fat: 31g

Cholesterol: 165mg

Sodium: 2,530mg

Carbs: 48g

Fiber: 5g

Sugars: 23g

Protein: 45g

Chicken, Vegetable & Matzo Ball Soup

This Passover favorite features unleavened matzo balls made with almond flour and potato starch. Similar to chicken noodle soup, but without the noodles, this warm rosemary seasoned soup is sure to bring a crowd to your table.

FOR THE MATZO BALL BATTER

2 ½ cups blanched almond flour

2 teaspoons kosher salt, divided

1 teaspoon potato starch

1 teaspoon garlic powder

1 teaspoon onion powder

4 large eggs

FOR THE CHICKEN AND VEGETABLE STOCK

1 tablespoon olive oil

1 cup diced carrots

1 cup diced onion

1 cup diced celery

10 cups chicken or vegetable stock

3 cups shredded cooked rotisserie chicken

1 teaspoon dried parsley

1 teaspoon dried rosemary

1 To make the matzo ball batter, in a large mixing bowl, combine almond flour, 1 teaspoon kosher salt, potato starch, garlic powder and onion powder. Mix together well.

2 In the bowl of a stand mixer using the paddle attachment, beat together eggs and remaining 1 teaspoon of kosher salt. Mix on medium speed until eggs are light and fluffy.

3 Add dry ingredients slowly to the wet ingredients, mixing on medium speed until well combined. Transfer matzo ball batter to a bowl, cover and refrigerate for 1 hour.

4 To make the chicken and vegetable stock, in a large pot, heat olive oil over medium heat. Add carrots, onions and celery and sauté until onions become translucent, but not browned, about 5 minutes. Add chicken or vegetable stock, rotisserie chicken, parsley and rosemary and bring to a slow boil.

5 Roll the chilled matzo ball batter into 12 equal-sized balls. Drop each ball in the boiling stock, cover and simmer for 20 minutes. If you like your matzo balls more firm, do not cover pot during this time.

6 Ladle soup into bowls and serve immediately.

NUTRITION PER SERVING

Calories: 620

Fat: 36g

Sat Fat: 5g

Cholesterol: 215mg

Sodium: 1,350mg

Carbs: 31g

Fiber: 6g

Sugars: 10g

Protein: 46g

Creamy Crab & Oyster Mushroom Bisque

YIELD
6 servings

PREP TIME
15 minutes

TOTAL TIME
50 minutes

Bisques are creamy French soups made with seafood and are often orangey in color, due to the addition of tomato paste. This one in particular uses crab and a type of gourmet mushroom that is thin and flat. For an extra layer of heartiness, serve this soup over rice. The soup cuts down on the calories by splitting the dairy content into part skim milk and part half and half.

2 tablespoons butter

1 pound sliced oyster mushrooms

2 shallots, finely diced

2 carrots, diced

3 cloves garlic, minced

½ cup sherry

1 (4 ounce) can tomato paste

2 teaspoons Worcestershire sauce

1 teaspoon paprika

1 teaspoon dried thyme

1 teaspoon Old Bay seasoning

2 teaspoons salt

2 cups fish stock

1 cup half and half

1 cup skim milk

1 ½ pounds crabmeat, cut into bite-sized chunks

Salt, to taste

1 In a large soup pot, heat butter over medium heat. Add oyster mushrooms, shallots and carrots and cook, stirring occasionally, until vegetables are soft, about 5 to 7 minutes. Add garlic and cook 1 additional minute until fragrant.

2 Add sherry and increase heat to medium-high. Bring liquid to a boil and let reduce by half.

3 Whisk in tomato paste, Worcestershire sauce, paprika, thyme, Old Bay seasoning and salt. Cook, stirring constantly, for 5 minutes. Add fish stock and bring mixture to a boil. Reduce heat to medium-low, cover and let simmer for 10 minutes. Whisk in half and half, skim milk and crabmeat and simmer for 8 to 10 minutes before serving. Season with additional salt, if desired. Serve immediately.

NUTRITION PER SERVING

Calories: 330

Fat: 11g

Sat Fat: 6g

Cholesterol: 90mg

Sodium: 1,940mg

Carbs: 24g

Fiber: 4g

Sugars: 10g

Protein: 30g

Watermelon, Heirloom Tomatoes & Mint Summer Salad

Forget lettuce and arugula. This juicy watermelon and colorful heirloom tomato savory fruit salad is just what you need to cool off during the hottest days of summer. With a refreshing mint garnish, all that's missing is a poolside chair and a tall glass of lemonade.

4 cups diced watermelon

2 cups diced heirloom tomatoes (a variety of colored tomatoes, if possible)

2 cups finely diced cucumber

¼ cup finely chopped red onion

¼ cup thinly sliced mint strips

2 tablespoons extra-virgin olive oil

1 teaspoon salt

1 In a salad or mixing bowl, combine watermelon, tomatoes, cucumber, red onion and mint.

2 Drizzle salad with olive oil and salt and mix just enough to combine. Cover and refrigerate for 1 hour before serving.

NUTRITION PER SERVING

Calories: 100

Fat: 5g

Sat Fat: 0.5g

Cholesterol: 0mg

Sodium: 520mg

Carbs: 14g

Fiber: 1g

Sugars: 10g

Protein: 2g

YIELD
6 servings

PREP TIME
10 minutes

TOTAL TIME
45 minutes

NUTRITION
PER SERVING

Calories: 540

Fat: 28g

Sat Fat: 5g

Cholesterol:
15mg

Sodium:
1,280mg

Carbs: 66g

Fiber: 12g

Sugars: 6g

Protein: 11g

Creamy Pasta Salad with Caramelized Mushrooms, Artichokes & Avocado

This pasta salad is sure to be a hit at the neighborhood block party. Caramelized button mushrooms and chopped artichoke hearts are tossed with freshly diced avocado and then mixed with penne. The creamy dairy-based dressing will keep your gluten-free pasta salad moist even after it's been refrigerated.

FOR THE PASTA SALAD

12 ounces gluten-free corn-based penne pasta

4 tablespoons extra-virgin olive oil, divided

1 pound thinly sliced button mushrooms

2 teaspoons sugar

1 teaspoon garlic powder

1 teaspoon salt

2 (14 ounce) cans artichoke hearts, chopped into bite-sized pieces

2 avocados, peeled, seeds removed and diced

FOR THE DRESSING

½ cup sour cream

¼ cup mayonnaise

2 teaspoons milk

2 teaspoons lemon juice

1 teaspoon paprika

1 teaspoon salt

1 teaspoon garlic powder

½ teaspoon dried mustard

1 To make the pasta salad, cook gluten-free pasta according to package instructions, adding 1 tablespoon olive oil to the water. When pasta is cooked, drain water and run the pasta under cold water. Set aside to finish cooling. Add 1 tablespoon olive oil to pasta while it's cooling to keep it from sticking together.

2 In a large skillet, heat remaining 2 tablespoons of olive oil over medium-high heat. Add mushrooms, sugar, garlic powder and salt and cook, stirring occasionally, until mushrooms are browned, about 7 minutes. Add artichokes and cook 3 additional minutes, stirring frequently. Remove vegetables from heat and cool completely.

3 To make the dressing, in a mixing bowl, whisk together sour cream, mayonnaise, milk, lemon juice, paprika, salt, garlic powder and dried mustard.

4 To assemble the salad, in a large bowl, toss together cooled pasta, mushrooms, artichokes and avocado. Pour dressing over the salad and, using a spatula, gently toss together to coat all elements well. Cover and refrigerate until ready to serve.

Cumin-Lime Spiced Brown Rice Taco Salad

Inspired by beef tacos, this Tex-Mex salad is an entrée to throw into your salad rotation. Seasoned ground beef and brown rice are tossed with lettuce, tomato and Monterey Jack cheese and topped with a cilantro-lime cream dressing. Cumin, the main spice in the dish, has a nutty and peppery flavor and is packed with iron.

YIELD
6 servings

PREP TIME
20 minutes

TOTAL TIME
35 minutes

FOR THE RICE AND BEEF

2 cups brown rice

1 tablespoon extra-virgin olive oil

1 pound lean ground beef

2 teaspoons salt

2 teaspoons ground cumin

1 teaspoon garlic powder

FOR THE SALAD AND DRESSING

¾ cup sour cream

¼ cup freshly chopped cilantro leaves

2 ½ tablespoons lime juice

1 teaspoon ground cumin

1 teaspoon sugar

½ teaspoon salt

¼ teaspoon chili powder

1 head shredded iceberg lettuce

1 cup sliced plum tomatoes

1 cup shredded Monterey Jack cheese

2 cups corn tortilla strips

1 To make the rice and beef, cook brown rice according to package instructions. Cool completely and set aside until ready to toss with salad.

2 In a large skillet, heat olive oil over medium-high heat. Add ground beef and cook, stirring occasionally until meat is well browned, about 7 to 10 minutes. Season with salt, cumin and garlic powder. Remove from heat and cool.

3 To make the dressing, in a small bowl, whisk together sour cream, cilantro, lime juice, cumin, sugar, salt and chili powder.

4 To assemble the salad, toss together cooled brown rice, ground beef, lettuce, tomatoes and Monterey Jack cheese. Toss salad with dressing and arrange in 6 individual serving bowls. Garnish each salad with corn tortilla strips.

NUTRITION PER SERVING

Calories: 390

Fat: 17g

Sat Fat: 8g

Cholesterol: 70mg

Sodium: 1,260mg

Carbs: 37g

Fiber: 4g

Sugars: 4g

Protein: 23g

Quinoa, Cucumber & Mango Salad with Sweet Cilantro Vinaigrette

A perfect side salad to a spice-rubbed chicken entrée, this light quinoa salad is tossed with fresh cucumbers, mango, scallions and a sweet and citrusy vinaigrette. Cucumbers and mangos are both great sources of vitamins A and C. Color-coordinate your plate using different colors of quinoa. The lighter varieties of the grain tend to have a more delicate flavor, whereas the darker varieties tend to boast a nutty and earthy taste.

FOR THE QUINOA

2 cups black, red or plain quinoa

2 cups water

2 cups vegetable stock

Ice

FOR THE SWEET CILANTRO VINAIGRETTE AND SALAD

1 cup fresh cilantro leaves

¼ cup orange juice

1 tablespoon lemon juice

1 tablespoon red wine vinegar

1 tablespoon brown sugar

½ cup extra-virgin olive oil

1 cucumber, finely diced

1 mango, peeled, seed removed and finely diced

3 scallions, finely chopped

1 To make the quinoa, in a medium-sized pot, combine quinoa, water and vegetable stock. Bring to a boil over medium-high heat. Reduce heat to medium, cover pot and allow to simmer until all the liquid is absorbed, about 20 to 25 minutes.

2 Remove from heat and transfer quinoa mixture into a mixing bowl that is sitting in an ice bath. Fluff quinoa mixture occasionally until fully cooled.

3 To make the sweet cilantro vinaigrette, in a food processor or blender, combine cilantro, orange juice, lemon juice, red wine vinegar, brown sugar and olive oil. Pulse until cilantro is finely minced and an emulsified vinaigrette forms.

4 To assemble the salad, in a large mixing bowl, combine cucumber, mango and scallions. Stir together gently and then add cooled quinoa mixture. Toss salad with sweet cilantro vinaigrette. Cover and refrigerate until ready to serve.

NUTRITION PER SERVING

Calories: 450

Fat: 23g

Sat Fat: 3.5g

Cholesterol: 0mg

Sodium: 125mg

Carbs: 53g

Fiber: 6g

Sugars: 13g

Protein: 11g

Gazpacho Salad

This raw salad is a mixture of tomato, cucumber, orange bell pepper and onion tossed in a simple lemon, red wine and olive oil vinaigrette. Although there are many colors of bell peppers, the "hotter" the color, the sweeter the flavor. If you can't find orange bell peppers, red ones will do. (See photo on pages 78–79)

YIELD
6 servings

PREP TIME
15 minutes

TOTAL TIME
20 minutes

1 In a large bowl, toss together tomatoes, cucumber, orange bell pepper, onions, cilantro and basil.

2 In a small bowl, whisk together olive oil, lemon juice, red wine vinegar, salt, sugar and garlic powder. Pour over vegetables and toss to combine. Serve immediately, or cover and refrigerate until ready to serve.

1 pound grape tomatoes, quartered

1 large cucumber, finely diced

1 orange bell pepper, seeds and pith removed, diced

½ cup finely diced sweet yellow onion

¼ cup finely chopped cilantro

2 tablespoons finely chopped basil

¼ cup extra-virgin olive oil

2 tablespoons lemon juice

1 tablespoon red wine vinegar

1 teaspoon salt

1 teaspoon sugar

½ teaspoon garlic powder

NUTRITION PER SERVING

Calories: 120

Fat: 10g

Sat Fat: 1.5g

Cholesterol: 0mg

Sodium: 390mg

Carbs: 8g

Fiber: 2g

Sugars: 4g

Protein: 1g

YIELD
6 servings

PREP TIME
15 minutes

TOTAL TIME
45 minutes

Caesar Salad with Avocado Dressing & Garlic Croutons

This twist on the traditional Caesar salad starts with the dressing. A light yet creamy vinaigrette made with avocado, garlic and Dijon mustard graces the chopped romaine lettuce and tomatoes. Don't forget to add the Parmesan cheese or the homemade gluten-free croutons! For the baguettes, we suggest using Against the Grain or Schar brand baguettes.

FOR THE CAESAR AVOCADO DRESSING

1 avocado, peeled and seed removed

4 cloves garlic

2 tablespoons mayonnaise

1 tablespoon Dijon mustard

1 tablespoon plus 1 teaspoon cider vinegar

2 ½ tablespoons lemon juice

1 teaspoon salt

¼ teaspoon pepper

½ cup extra-virgin olive oil

FOR THE CROUTONS

3 tablespoons butter

1 teaspoon garlic powder

1 teaspoon paprika

½ teaspoon onion powder

½ teaspoon salt

1 gluten-free baguette, cut into bite-sized cubes (about 3 heaping cups)

FOR THE SALAD

1 head romaine lettuce, chopped into bite-sized pieces

1 cup shaved or grated Parmesan cheese

1 cup cherry tomatoes, sliced in half

1 To make the Caesar avocado dressing, in a food processor or blender, combine avocado, garlic, mayonnaise, Dijon mustard, cider vinegar, lemon juice, salt and pepper. Pulse until a smooth purée forms. Drizzle in olive oil while running the food processor until an emulsified dressing forms. Cover and refrigerate until ready to use.

2 To make the croutons, in a large nonstick skillet, heat butter over medium-high heat. Stir in garlic powder, paprika, onion powder and salt. Add bread pieces and toss to coat each piece in the butter seasoning mixture. Sauté until bread pieces begin to brown, about 5 to 7 minutes. Remove from pan and cool completely.

3 To assemble the salad, toss together romaine lettuce, Parmesan cheese, cherry tomatoes and croutons. Drizzle desired amount of Caesar avocado dressing on top of salad and toss to coat all ingredients. Serve immediately or cover and refrigerate until ready to serve.

NUTRITION PER SERVING

Calories: 760

Fat: 56g

Sat Fat: 12g

Cholesterol: 30mg

Sodium: 1,070mg

Carbs: 63g

Fiber: 15g

Sugars: 6g

Protein: 13g

White & Milk Chocolate Fruit Kebabs – page 117

YIELD
4 servings

PREP TIME
10 minutes

TOTAL TIME
25 minutes

Old Bay Spiced Kale Chips

Lacinato kale, also known as "dinosaur kale," is the Italian cultivar of the familiar curly kale. It's blue-green in color with embossed leaves that look like dinosaur scales. Thicker than the curly kale variety, it requires more cooking time. You can use another kind of kale, but be sure to keep an eye on it in the oven so it doesn't burn.

Parchment paper, for lining baking sheets

1 bunch lacinato kale, stems removed and torn into large pieces (or any kale your store has available—adjust cooking time for thinner kale varieties)

1 tablespoon olive oil

1 teaspoon Old Bay seasoning

½ teaspoon salt

1 Preheat oven to 350°F. Line 3 baking sheets with parchment paper and set aside.

2 Make sure kale is very dry—pat dry with paper towels and let air-dry if necessary.

3 Place kale into a large bowl. Drizzle olive oil over kale and "massage" into kale until evenly coated. Add Old Bay seasoning and salt and toss to combine.

4 Bake for 12 to 15 minutes until dark and crispy. Let cool slightly before serving.

NUTRITION PER SERVING

Calories: 110

Fat: 4.5g

Sat Fat: 0.5g

Cholesterol: 0mg

Sodium: 810mg

Carbs: 17g

Fiber: 3g

Sugars: 0g

Protein: 6g

YIELD
12 servings

PREP TIME
5 minutes

TOTAL TIME
30 minutes

Edamame Guacamole with Pecorino & Lemon Zest

In this dish, nutritional powerhouses like edamame and avocado come together with buttery and nutty Pecorino cheese. This bright green dip is a great party appetizer when served with crackers or chips, but it's equally good on a toasted gluten-free baguette. Be sure to purchase frozen edamame peas that are already out of their shells to save yourself the time of deshelling the peas.

Water, for boiling

3 cups frozen edamame peas

2 ½ tablespoons salt, divided

2 avocados, peeled and seeds removed

½ cup mint

3 tablespoons lemon juice

1 tablespoon lemon zest

1 cup grated Pecorino cheese plus additional shaved Pecorino cheese for topping

1 gluten-free baguette, sliced and toasted

1 Bring a medium pot of water to a boil and add edamame peas and ½ tablespoon salt. Cook for 4 minutes. Drain and let cool.

2 Add edamame peas to a food processor and pulse for 30 seconds or until smooth. Be sure to scrape down sides. Add avocado, mint, lemon juice, lemon zest, grated Pecorino cheese and remaining salt to edamame peas and pulse until well blended. Transfer to a bowl, cover and refrigerate until ready to serve.

3 Toast gluten-free baguette slices and spread a heaping spoonful of dip onto each slice. Top with shaved Pecorino cheese and serve.

NUTRITION PER SERVING

Calories: 280

Fat: 18g

Sat Fat: 4g

Cholesterol: 15mg

Sodium: 1,720mg

Carbs: 25g

Fiber: 7g

Sugars: 3g

Protein: 9g

Honey Buttered Pretzel Bites with Cheddar Cheese & Beer Dip

Who needs pretzels from the mall when you can make them at home? These sweet and salty honey butter–brushed pretzel bites are a great movie night snack, especially when served with a warm cheddar cheese and beer dip. For this particular recipe, we recommend using a gluten-free lager beer like Bard's Beer.

FOR THE PRETZEL BITES

Parchment paper and nonstick cooking spray, for lining and greasing baking sheet

1 ½ cups warm water

1 tablespoon sugar

2 teaspoons salt

2 ¼ teaspoons (1 package) rapid-rise yeast

1 egg

4 cups gluten-free all-purpose flour

8 tablespoons (1 stick) butter, melted and divided

Olive oil, for greasing bowl

Water, for boiling

¼ cup baking soda

1 tablespoon honey

1 tablespoon coarse salt

FOR THE CHEDDAR CHEESE AND BEER DIP

2 (8 ounce) blocks cream cheese

2 cups shredded sharp cheddar cheese

½ cup gluten-free beer

⅛ teaspoon salt

1 Preheat oven to 375°F. Line a baking sheet with parchment paper and spray with nonstick cooking spray and set aside.

2 To make the pretzel bites, in the bowl of a stand mixer using the paddle attachement, combine warm water, sugar, salt and yeast. Let mixture sit until it becomes foamy, about 5 to 7 minutes.

3 Add egg and mix well. Add gluten-free all-purpose flour and 4 tablespoons melted butter and mix until a smooth dough forms.

4 Rub a large mixing bowl with olive oil and transfer dough to the bowl. Cover and let dough rise in a warm place for 30 minutes.

5 Fill a large pot with water and add baking soda. Heat over high heat until it comes to a boil.

6 Roll dough into thick breadsticks and then cut dough into bite-sized pieces. Carefully drop each pretzel bite into boiling water for about 30 seconds. Remove from water and place on prepared baking sheet. Repeat until all dough is boiled.

7 In a small bowl, whisk together 4 tablespoons of melted butter and honey. Brush each pretzel bite with mixture and then sprinkle coarse salt on top. Bake for 20 to 25 minutes until pretzels are golden brown.

8 To make the cheddar cheese and beer dip, in a saucepan over medium heat, heat cream cheese and cheddar cheese. Whisk constantly until cream cheese is mostly melted, about 5 minutes. Add beer and whisk until smooth. Cook, whisking frequently for another 3 minutes until gently simmering. Season with salt. Serve with pretzel bites.

Herbed Hummus

YIELD
8 servings

PREP TIME
5 minutes

TOTAL TIME
10 minutes

Quite possibly one of the simplest recipes in this book! Simply blend and serve. Hummus is a Middle Eastern appetizer or side dish made from puréed garbanzo beans, otherwise known as chickpeas, with tahini, olive oil, lemon and garlic. *Delight*'s version ups the ante with a medley of herbs, including basil, cilantro, parsley and chives.

1 (15 ounce) can no-salt-added garbanzo beans, rinsed and drained

2 tablespoons tahini (sesame paste)

⅛ cup water

1 tablespoon olive oil

3 tablespoons lemon juice

1 cup fresh basil leaves

1 cup fresh cilantro leaves

1 cup fresh parsley

½ cup fresh chives

2 cloves garlic

1 teaspoon salt

1 In a food processor, combine garbanzo beans, tahini, water, olive oil, lemon juice, basil, cilantro, parsley, chives, garlic and salt. Pulse until a smooth hummus mixture forms. Add additional olive oil to thin the mixture, if necessary.

2 Serve with freshly sliced vegetables, tortilla chips or gluten-free bread.

NUTRITION PER SERVING

Calories: 100

Fat: 5g

Sat Fat: 0.5g

Cholesterol: 0mg

Sodium: 420mg

Carbs: 11g

Fiber: 3g

Sugars: 1g

Protein: 4g

YIELD
4 servings

PREP TIME
5 minutes

TOTAL TIME
1 hour
15 minutes

Roasted Seasoned Chickpeas

Chickpeas, also known as garbanzo beans, are a good source of fiber and protein. When seasoned and roasted with a little sesame oil, garlic powder and sea salt, they have a delightfully crunchy texture and are great for a healthy midday snack attack.

Foil, for lining baking sheet

2 (15 ounce) cans chickpeas, rinsed and drained

1 tablespoon sesame oil

1 teaspoon garlic powder

½ teaspoon sea salt

1 Preheat oven to 300°F. Line a baking sheet with foil and set aside.

2 Pat dry chickpeas to remove any excess water. Place chickpeas in a single layer on the prepared baking sheet. Dry-roast chickpeas for 1 hour. Be sure to give baking sheet a shake every 15 minutes to prevent them from burning.

3 Remove from oven and toss chickpeas in a bowl with sesame oil, garlic powder and sea salt. Increase oven temperature to 375°F.

4 Return chickpeas to prepared baking sheet and bake for another 10 minutes at 375°F.

5 Remove from oven and let chickpeas cool completely before serving.

**NUTRITION
PER SERVING**

Calories: 200

Fat: 6g

Sat Fat: 0g

Cholesterol: 0mg

Sodium: 760mg

Carbs: 29g

Fiber: 7g

Sugars: 3g

Protein: 8g

YIELD
6 servings

PREP TIME
10 minutes

TOTAL TIME
30 minutes

Hot & Creamy Crab Dip

This sinfully sweet crab dip, mixed with a creamy blend of cheeses, lemon and Old Bay seasoning, is so deliciously rich, you'll want to eat it all in one sitting. This is a great snack or hors d'oeuvre, especially when you serve it on gluten-free crackers.

Nonstick cooking spray, for greasing the baking dish

8 ounces cream cheese, softened

1 cup mayonnaise

½ cup shredded sharp cheddar cheese

2 scallions, minced

1 shallot, finely minced

½ tablespoon Worcestershire sauce

2 teaspoons Old Bay seasoning

1 teaspoon lemon juice

½ teaspoon salt

½ teaspoon pepper

½ teaspoon garlic powder

1 (8 ounce) container fresh jumbo lump crabmeat

½ cup freshly grated Parmesan cheese

1 Preheat oven to 400°F. Spray a 1 ½-quart round baking dish with nonstick cooking spray and set aside.

2 In a large mixing bowl, stir together cream cheese, mayonnaise, cheddar cheese, scallions, shallots, Worcestershire sauce, Old Bay seasoning, lemon juice, salt, pepper and garlic powder. Gently fold in crabmeat.

3 Transfer mixture to prepared baking dish and top with Parmesan cheese.

4 Bake for 15 to 20 minutes, until bubbly and golden. Serve with fresh vegetables, tortilla chips or gluten-free bread.

NUTRITION PER SERVING

Calories: 400

Fat: 32g

Sat Fat: 12g

Cholesterol: 90mg

Sodium: 1,250mg

Carbs: 13g

Fiber: 0g

Sugars: 4g

Protein: 16g

Smokey Hot Spinach Dip

This decadent comfort food may be served as a dip with tortilla chips or used as a spread on toasted gluten-free bread slices.

1 tablespoon olive oil

½ cup chopped red onion

½ teaspoon salt, divided

10 ounces frozen spinach, thawed and chopped

1 ½ teaspoons Worcestershire sauce

½ teaspoon hot sauce

1 teaspoon minced garlic

1 teaspoon smoked paprika plus additional for garnish

4 ounces cream cheese

7 ounces Greek yogurt

4 ounces shredded smoked cheddar cheese

¼ teaspoon black pepper

1 In a pan over medium heat, add olive oil, red onion and ¼ teaspoon salt. Sauté for 7 minutes, then add spinach and cook for another 5 minutes until spinach is heated through.

2 Add Worcestershire sauce, hot sauce, garlic and smoked paprika to the pan and cook for an additional minute, stirring frequently.

3 Stir in cream cheese, Greek yogurt and smoked cheddar cheese. Continue stirring until cheese has melted fully. Stir in remaining ¼ teaspoon of salt and pepper.

4 Transfer dip into a serving bowl, dust the top with smoked paprika and serve warm with tortilla chips or spread on toasted gluten-free bread slices.

YIELD
4 servings

PREP TIME
10 minutes

TOTAL TIME
25 minutes

NUTRITION PER SERVING

Calories: 340

Fat: 28g

Sat Fat: 15g

Cholesterol: 70mg

Sodium: 670mg

Carbs: 10g

Fiber: 3g

Sugars: 4g

Protein: 15g

White Bean Artichoke Dip

A serving of this dip with a side of freshly cut mixed vegetables is a tasty way to reach your 5-a-day servings of vegetables and fruits.

2 tablespoons olive oil, divided

½ cup chopped red onion

1 teaspoon salt, divided

4 tablespoons plus ½ cup water

1 cup frozen artichoke hearts, thawed and chopped

1 teaspoon minced garlic

1 teaspoon fresh thyme leaves

⅛ teaspoon red chili flakes

1 (15 ounce) can Great Northern beans, rinsed and drained

2 tablespoons freshly squeezed lemon juice

Chopped scallions, for garnish

1 In a skillet over medium-low heat, add 1 tablespoon olive oil.

2 Add red onion and ¼ teaspoon salt to skillet and toss to coat in olive oil. Cook onions for 7 minutes, adding 4 tablespoons water as onions cook to prevent them from browning.

3 Add artichokes to the skillet and cook an additional 5 minutes.

4 To the artichoke mixture, add garlic, thyme and red chili flakes and cook 1 additional minute until fragrant.

5 Remove mixture from the heat. Measure out 3 tablespoons of mixture from the skillet and set aside.

6 To the artichoke mixture remaining in the skillet, stir in beans, ½ cup water, lemon juice and remaining ¾ teaspoon of salt and stir to combine. Place this mixture in a blender or food processor and pulse until smooth.

7 Spoon dip into a serving bowl and top with reserved artichoke mixture. Cover and refrigerate for 30 minutes to chill. Sprinkle chopped scallions on top before serving.

8 Serve with fresh-cut vegetables and/or gluten-free crackers.

NUTRITION PER SERVING

Calories: 120

Fat: 5g

Sat Fat: 0.5g

Cholesterol: 0mg

Sodium: 780mg

Carbs: 15g

Fiber: 5g

Sugars: 1g

Protein: 5g

YIELD
4 servings

PREP TIME
15 minutes

TOTAL TIME
1 hour
15 minutes

Wasabi Chicken Salad Lettuce Wraps

Portable and protein-packed, this savory salad is served on large crunchy butter lettuce leaves. Adjust the amount of wasabi to suit the level of heat you like.

2 cups shredded rotisserie chicken, skin removed

1 cup shredded cucumbers

1 cup shredded carrots

1 bunch chopped green onions, roots trimmed off

3 tablespoons rice vinegar

1 tablespoon sesame oil

2 teaspoons gluten-free Tamari soy sauce

1 teaspoon wasabi powder

1 ½ teaspoons dark brown sugar

1 teaspoon minced garlic

1 teaspoon grated fresh ginger

1 teaspoon toasted sesame seeds

1 head butter lettuce

1 In a large bowl, toss together rotisserie chicken, cucumbers, carrots and green onions.

2 In a separate bowl, whisk together rice vinegar, sesame oil, gluten-free soy sauce, wasabi powder, brown sugar, garlic, ginger and sesame seeds.

3 Pour dressing over the chicken mixture. Using your hands, toss ingredients together until well mixed. Cover and refrigerate at least 1 hour before serving.

4 Remove large whole leaves from the butter lettuce and place on a plate.

5 Place chicken salad in the center of lettuce leaves to serve.

NUTRITION PER SERVING

Calories: 240

Fat: 8g

Sat Fat: 1.5g

Cholesterol: 70mg

Sodium: 610mg

Carbs: 16g

Fiber: 5g

Sugars: 9g

Protein: 30g

YIELD
8 servings

PREP TIME
10 minutes

TOTAL TIME
20 minutes

Sriracha & Brown Sugared Nuts

This simple combination comes together quickly for a satisfying and addictive snack.

Parchment paper, for lining baking sheet

1 tablespoon Sriracha chili sauce

3 tablespoons dark brown sugar

2 teaspoons gluten-free Tamari soy sauce

1 teaspoon olive oil

2 cups unsalted roasted cashews

1 Line a baking sheet with parchment paper and set aside.

2 In a small bowl, whisk together Sriracha, brown sugar, gluten-free soy sauce and olive oil. Pour mixture into a skillet and heat over medium heat until the mixture begins to bubble and thicken, about 2 to 3 minutes.

3 Add cashews to the skillet and stir to coat nuts evenly in the sauce.

4 Remove from heat and scatter nuts onto prepared baking sheet. As nuts cool to the touch, separate them from clusters into individual pieces.

5 Let nuts cool completely before storing in an airtight container.

NUTRITION PER SERVING

Calories: 220

Fat: 16g

Sat Fat: 3g

Cholesterol: 0mg

Sodium: 85mg

Carbs: 16g

Fiber: 1g

Sugars: 6g

Protein: 5g

YIELD
2 servings

PREP TIME
5 minutes

TOTAL TIME
35 minutes

Chocolate Yogurt Fruit Dip

When a chocolate craving strikes, satisfy it in a healthier way than reaching for a candy bar. Low-fat Greek yogurt is thick, creamy and rich in protein and calcium. Combined with melted chocolate chips, this fruit dip is a luxurious treat for a late afternoon pick-me-up.

¼ cup mini chocolate chips

1 teaspoon orange zest

2 teaspoons water

½ teaspoon vanilla extract

1 (7 ounce) container 2% Greek yogurt

Chopped chocolate chips and grated orange zest, for garnish

1 In a microwave-safe bowl, toss together chocolate chips, orange zest and water. Place in microwave and heat for 10 seconds at 50% power, stir chips and repeat process 2 more times until fully melted.

2 Remove mixture from the microwave and stir in vanilla extract.

3 Add Greek yogurt and whisk well to combine with all ingredients. Sprinkle chopped chocolate chips and grated orange zest on top. Cover and refrigerate for 30 minutes before serving with fruit.

NUTRITION PER SERVING

Calories: 170

Fat: 8g

Sat Fat: 5g

Cholesterol: 5mg

Sodium: 35mg

Carbs: 18g

Fiber: 1g

Sugars: 16g

Protein: 9g

YIELD
8 servings

PREP TIME
10 minutes

TOTAL TIME
2 hours

Caramel Apple Rounds

Oven-baked apple rounds topped with cinnamon and drizzled with a caramel sauce. For a variation in flavor, try using several apple types. Granny Smith apples will give you a more tart flavor, while Gala or Golden Delicious apples will be much sweeter.

FOR THE CARAMEL SAUCE

Parchment paper, for lining baking sheets

1 ½ cups granulated sugar

½ cup salted butter

¾ cup heavy whipping cream, room temperature

FOR THE APPLES

3 Red Delicious apples, cored and thinly sliced

2 tablespoons ground cinnamon

1 Preheat oven to 200°F. Line 2 baking sheets with parchment paper and set aside.

2 To make the caramel sauce, in a saucepan over medium heat, add sugar. Whisk sugar until melted. Once it has reached a dark amber color, stir in butter. Continue to whisk until butter has melted. Remove from heat and gradually pour in heavy whipping cream. Stir until smooth. Let cool and set aside.

3 To make the apples, arrange slices neatly on prepared baking sheets. Sprinkle with cinnamon and bake for 1 hour.

4 Remove baking sheets from the oven and drizzle apple slices with caramel sauce. Return to oven for 30 to 40 minutes or until apple slices have absorbed most of the caramel sauce. Let cool before serving.

NUTRITION PER SERVING

Calories: 370

Fat: 20g

Sat Fat: 13g

Cholesterol: 60mg

Sodium: 110mg

Carbs: 52g

Fiber: 3g

Sugars: 46g

Protein: 1g

YIELD
4 servings

PREP TIME
10 minutes

TOTAL TIME
1 hour

NUTRITION PER SERVING

Calories: 710

Fat: 27g

Sat Fat: 5g

Cholesterol: 0mg

Sodium: 110mg

Carbs: 99g

Fiber: 9g

Sugars: 60g

Protein: 20g

Homemade Granola Berry Crunch Parfait

A healthy combination of homemade granola, berries and Greek yogurt. Add a sweet kick to these parfaits with honey or agave nectar.

FOR THE GRANOLA

Parchment paper, for lining baking sheet

2 cups gluten-free rolled oats

½ cup brown sugar

⅓ cup shredded unsweetened coconut flakes

⅓ cup crushed cashews

¼ cup flax meal

¼ cup vegetable oil

¼ cup warm water

1 tablespoon vanilla extract

FOR THE PARFAITS

1 cup sliced fresh strawberries

¾ cup fresh blueberries

16 ounces nonfat vanilla Greek yogurt

¼ cup honey or agave nectar

1 Preheat oven to 325°F. Line a baking sheet with parchment paper and set aside.

2 To make the granola, in a large bowl, combine gluten-free oats, brown sugar, coconut flakes, cashews and flax meal. Stir until mixed thoroughly. Add vegetable oil, warm water and vanilla extract. Continue to stir until well combined. Spread granola evenly onto prepared baking sheet.

3 Bake for 45 minutes or until golden, stirring every 15 minutes. Remove from oven and let cool before preparing the parfaits.

4 To make the parfaits, arrange parfaits in 4 glasses by layering granola, berries and Greek yogurt to your liking. Drizzle with honey or agave nectar before serving.

YIELD
10 servings

PREP TIME
10 minutes

TOTAL TIME
1 hour

Chocolate-Dipped Pretzels

Gluten-free pretzels dipped in chocolate and sprinkled with a blend of nuts. Cashews, macadamia nuts and shredded coconut add a nice twist to this flavorful recipe.

Parchment paper, for lining baking sheet
½ cup salted macadamia nuts
½ cup salted cashews
⅓ cup shredded unsweetened coconut flakes
2 tablespoons granulated sugar
1 (12 ounce) package milk chocolate morsels
¼ cup water
14 ounces gluten-free pretzels

1 Line a baking sheet with parchment paper and set aside.

2 In a food processor, crush macadamia nuts and cashews. Add coconut flakes and sugar. Continue to process until all ingredients are finely crushed.

3 Transfer nut blend into a bowl and set aside.

4 In a medium saucepan over medium heat, add chocolate morsels and water. Stir until chocolate has melted completely. Remove from heat.

5 Dip pretzels into melted chocolate and then sprinkle with the crushed nut blend. Place dipped pretzels onto prepared baking sheet to prevent them from sticking.

6 Place dipped pretzels in refrigerator until chocolate has fully hardened.

NUTRITION PER SERVING

Calories: 460

Fat: 27g

Sat Fat: 10g

Cholesterol: 0mg

Sodium: 50mg

Carbs: 56g

Fiber: 4g

Sugars: 23g

Protein: 4g

YIELD
20 servings

PREP TIME
10 minutes

TOTAL TIME
30 minutes

Zesty Corn Fritters

Crisp corn fritters made from cornmeal and deep-fried to perfection. Served with a simple dipping sauce.

FOR THE CORN FRITTERS

2 ¼ cups cornmeal

½ teaspoon garlic powder

½ teaspoon parsley flakes

2 cups water, for boiling

¼ cup granulated sugar

1 tablespoon butter

1 teaspoon salt

2 cups vegetable oil

FOR THE DIPPING SAUCE

⅓ cup mayonnaise

⅓ cup ketchup

1 To make the corn fritters, in a large bowl, combine cornmeal, garlic powder and parsley flakes.

2 In a large saucepan, bring water to a boil. Add sugar, butter and salt. Stir until butter has melted completely. Turn heat to a low setting and gradually add the cornmeal mixture, stirring until it thickens. Let cool before handling.

3 Scoop 2 tablespoons of the dough and shape fritters by forming a ball and rolling it into a stick shape, about 3-inches long. Set aside on a plate. Repeat until all dough has been used.

4 Heat vegetable oil and fry each fritter until golden on all sides. Remove fritters from oil and drain any excess oil on paper towels.

5 To make the dipping sauce, combine mayonnaise and ketchup. Whisk until smooth. Serve sauce with fritters.

YIELD
20 servings

PREP TIME
10 minutes

TOTAL TIME
40 minutes

Easy Cheesy Snack Bites

A delicious snack made effortlessly using corn flour, potato flour and cheese. For a variation in flavor, substitute the cheese blend with other cheese types.

Parchment paper, for lining baking sheets

1 cup corn flour

½ cup potato flour

2 teaspoons granulated sugar

¼ teaspoon salt

2 cups Mexican cheese blend (cheddar and Monterey Jack)

1 cup warm water

2 eggs, beaten

1 Preheat oven to 400°F. Line several baking sheets with parchment paper and set aside.

2 In the bowl of a stand mixer using the paddle attachment, combine corn flour, potato flour, sugar and salt. Add cheese blend and mix thoroughly. Add warm water and eggs and continue to mix until a smooth dough has formed.

3 Drop dough by tablespoonful onto prepared baking sheets. Bake for 25 minutes or until slightly golden. Cool slightly before serving.

NUTRITION PER SERVING

Calories: 80

Fat: 4g

Sat Fat: 2g

Cholesterol: 30mg

Sodium: 115mg

Carbs: 9g

Fiber: 1g

Sugars: 1g

Protein: 4g

Sweet Pineapple Dip

YIELD
20 servings

PREP TIME
10 minutes

TOTAL TIME
20 minutes

Did you think Spam was a thing of the past? Think again! This recipe contains the flavorful blend of spiced ham and cream cheese topped with sweet pineapple preserves. Serve with gluten-free crackers.

1 (12 ounce) can Spam

1 (8 ounce) package cream cheese, softened

¾ cup pineapple preserves

1 In a food processor, combine Spam and cream cheese.

2 Transfer mixture to a bowl and top with pineapple preserves.

3 Serve with gluten-free crackers.

NUTRITION PER SERVING

Calories: 120

Fat: 9g

Sat Fat: 14g

Cholesterol: 25mg

Sodium: 270mg

Carbs: 9g

Fiber: 0g

Sugars: 8g

Protein: 3g

White & Milk Chocolate Fruit Kebabs

Nutritious kebabs made with strawberries, kiwi, cantaloupe, pineapple, grapes and blueberries. The fruit is dipped in chocolate and topped with peanuts and shredded coconut. (See photo on pages 94–95)

YIELD
8 servings

PREP TIME
10 minutes

TOTAL TIME
30 minutes

Parchment paper, for lining baking sheet

8 fresh strawberries, stems removed

2 kiwis, peeled and sliced

1 cup cantaloupe, cubed

½ cup pineapple, cubed

½ cup red seedless grapes

¼ cup fresh blueberries

1 (12 ounce) package white chocolate morsels

½ cup water, divided

1 (12 ounce) package milk chocolate morsels

¼ cup crushed peanuts

¼ cup shredded unsweetened coconut

8 skewers

1 Rinse all fruit thoroughly and place on paper towels to remove excess water. Line a baking sheet with parchment paper and set aside.

2 In a saucepan, melt white chocolate morsels with ¼ cup water over medium heat. Stir until smooth. In a separate saucepan, repeat the same process with the milk chocolate morsels. Leave chocolate over very low heat to keep it melted.

3 Dip strawberries and kiwi into chocolate, alternating between white and milk chocolate and then place them on prepared baking sheet to prevent them from sticking.

4 Top with peanuts and coconut. Refrigerate for a few minutes, allowing chocolate-dipped fruit to harden slightly.

5 Arrange fruit kebabs by threading fruit onto the skewers to your liking and transfer them onto prepared baking sheet. Place in refrigerator until chocolate has fully hardened.

NUTRITION PER SERVING

Calories: 540

Fat: 30g

Sat Fat: 17g

Cholesterol: 20mg

Sodium: 80mg

Carbs: 63g

Fiber: 4g

Sugars: 56g

Protein: 8g

YIELD
4 servings

PREP TIME
10 minutes

TOTAL TIME
40 minutes

Baked Potato Chips with Parsley, Garlic & Sea Salt

Thinly sliced russet potatoes are coated with a blend of olive oil, garlic, minced parsley and sea salt. Oven-baked to perfection! This basic recipe can be spiced up with other flavors like Old Bay seasoning, curry powder or even chili powder for a hot bite!

NUTRITION PER SERVING

Calories: 210

Fat: 14g

Sat Fat: 2g

Cholesterol: 0mg

Sodium: 150mg

Carbs: 20g

Fiber: 2g

Sugars: 1g

Protein: 2g

Parchment paper, for lining baking sheets

¼ cup olive oil

½ tablespoon minced garlic

1 teaspoon dried parsley flakes

1 teaspoon sea salt

3 thinly sliced russet potatoes

1 Preheat oven to 400°F. Line 2 baking sheets with parchment paper and set aside.

2 In a small bowl, whisk together olive oil, garlic, parsley and sea salt.

3 Arrange potato slices neatly on prepared baking sheets. Drizzle olive oil mixture evenly over the potatoes. Bake for 30 minutes or until crisp. Remove from oven and let cool before serving.

Alfredo Popcorn

Do you love the taste of cheesy Alfredo pasta sauce, but hate all of the calories? Lighten up while still enjoying the essence of rich flavors with our freshly popped popcorn tossed with a blend of butter, Parmesan cheese, garlic powder and sea salt.

YIELD
10 servings

PREP TIME
10 minutes

TOTAL TIME
20 minutes

FOR THE POPCORN

¼ cup vegetable oil

1 cup popcorn kernels

FOR THE ALFREDO BLEND

¼ cup butter, melted

½ cup grated Parmesan cheese

1 teaspoon garlic powder

1 teaspoon sea salt

1 To make the popcorn, in a large pot over medium heat, add vegetable oil and 5 popcorn kernels. Cover pot and wait for the 5 kernels to pop. Once they start popping, add remaining popcorn kernels and stir until they are evenly coated with the heated vegetable oil. Cover pot and wait for the popcorn kernels to pop completely.

2 Once fully popped, transfer popcorn to a large bowl, let cool and set aside.

3 To make the Alfredo blend, in a small bowl, whisk together melted butter, Parmesan cheese, garlic powder and sea salt. Drizzle popcorn with the blend and toss until evenly coated.

NUTRITION PER SERVING

Calories: 160

Fat: 11g

Sat Fat: 3.5g

Cholesterol: 10mg

Sodium: 105mg

Carbs: 17g

Fiber: 3g

Sugars: 0g

Protein: 2g

CHAPTER FIVE

Vegetables & Side Dishes

Spicy Orange Sesame Carrots – page 139

YIELD
6 servings

PREP TIME
10 minutes

TOTAL TIME
1 hour
25 minutes

Green Apples with Chilled Roasted Brussels Sprouts & White Cheddar

This combination sounds funny, but it is truly amazing. The roasted Brussels sprouts have a little bit of a charred flavor to them, paired with crisp yet juicy apples and then tossed with sharp cheddar cheese. A great way to un–Brussels sprouts your Brussels sprouts! Your family will love the combination of flavors and they'll get a great boost of vitamins A, C, K and B_6.

FOR THE BRUSSELS SPROUTS AND APPLES

Foil, for lining the baking sheet

1 (12 ounce) package Brussels sprouts, stems removed and sliced in quarters

2 tablespoons olive oil

1 teaspoon salt

1 teaspoon garlic powder

2 green apples, skin on, cored and diced

8 ounce block sharp white cheddar cheese, diced into bite-sized cubes

FOR THE DRESSING

2 tablespoons freshly squeezed orange juice

2 tablespoons lemon juice

2 tablespoons lime juice

1 tablespoon red wine vinegar

½ teaspoon salt

½ teaspoon garlic powder

¼ teaspoon pepper

¼ cup olive oil

1 Preheat oven to 400°F. Line a baking sheet with foil.

2 To make the Brussels sprouts and apples, arrange Brussels sprouts evenly upon baking sheet. Drizzle sprouts with olive oil, salt and garlic powder and toss to evenly coat. Roast for 20 to 25 minutes until the sprouts are lightly golden and crisp. Remove from oven and cool completely.

3 In a large mixing bowl, toss together green apples, cheese and cooled Brussels sprouts.

4 To make the dressing, in a separate bowl, whisk together orange juice, lemon juice, lime juice, red wine vinegar, salt, garlic powder and pepper. Slowly whisk in olive oil until the mixture emulsifies. Pour dressing over the sprouts, apples and cheese mixture and gently toss together. Cover and chill for 1 hour before serving.

NUTRITION PER SERVING

Calories: 510

Fat: 40g

Sat Fat: 13g

Cholesterol: 60mg

Sodium: 1,250mg

Carbs: 29g

Fiber: 6g

Sugars: 15g

Protein: 18g

Vegetable Ribbons with Balsamic Dressing

This vegetable recipe is so simple yet impressive. Zucchini and squash are high in vitamin C, and a serving of carrots is 428 percent of your daily value for vitamin A. Just thinly slice green zucchini, yellow squash and carrots and then toss them with a creamy balsamic dressing.

FOR THE VEGETABLE RIBBONS

2 large zucchini

1 large yellow squash

4 carrots

1 bunch scallions, roots removed, whites and greens finely chopped

FOR THE CREAMY BALSAMIC DRESSING

¼ cup heavy cream

¼ cup plus 1 tablespoon balsamic vinegar

½ teaspoon garlic powder

½ teaspoon salt

1 Wash and trim the tops and bottoms off the zucchini and squash. Peel the carrots.

2 To make the vegetable ribbons, in a food processor using the shredder attachment, run the zucchini, squash and carrots through to slice into equally long thin strips. If you don't have a food processor, carefully cut all vegetables into long thin slices.

3 In a large mixing bowl, toss vegetables with chopped scallions.

4 To make the creamy balsamic dressing, in a small bowl, whisk together cream, balsamic vinegar, garlic powder and salt. Drizzle dressing over the vegetables and toss to combine. Serve immediately.

YIELD
6 servings

PREP TIME
10 minutes

TOTAL TIME
30 minutes

NUTRITION PER SERVING

Calories: 150

Fat: 6g

Sat Fat: 3.5g

Cholesterol: 20mg

Sodium: 360mg

Carbs: 22g

Fiber: 5g

Sugars: 14g

Protein: 5g

YIELD
6 servings

PREP TIME
5 minutes

TOTAL TIME
20 minutes

Cinnamon Scalloped Apples

Trade out your usual applesauce for these cinnamon Golden Delicious apples cooked with a dash of brandy. A sweet and tart side dish that goes great with baked chicken or pork chops. Not to mention, apples are a great source of antioxidants that are heart healthy. An apple a day . . .

3 tablespoons butter

5 Golden Delicious apples, cored and diced

¼ cup sugar

2 tablespoons cornstarch

2 teaspoons ground cinnamon

¼ teaspoon salt

2 tablespoons brandy (apple or pear brandy works best)

1 tablespoon lemon juice

1 In a large nonstick skillet, heat butter over medium heat. Add apples and cook, stirring occasionally, until apples are soft, about 5 to 7 minutes.

2 In a small bowl, mix together sugar, cornstarch, cinnamon and salt. Sprinkle mixture over the apples and mix well.

3 Add brandy and lemon juice and cook, stirring occasionally, until a thick sauce forms around the apples, about 3 to 5 minutes. Serve immediately.

NUTRITION PER SERVING

Calories: 220

Fat: 6g

Sat Fat: 3.5g

Cholesterol: 15mg

Sodium: 150mg

Carbs: 40g

Fiber: 5g

Sugars: 24g

Protein: 1g

YIELD
12 latkes
(2 latkes
per serving)

PREP TIME
10 minutes

TOTAL TIME
30 minutes

Parmesan Potato Latkes

Latkes, otherwise known as potato pancakes, are traditionally eaten during Hanukkah but aren't just for holiday celebrations. Try these cheesy potato cakes with a fried or poached egg on top for an easy and delicious brunch, or with smoked salmon and a sprig of dill as a simple appetizer.

3 russet potatoes
(approximately 2 pounds),
peeled and shredded

1 yellow onion, peeled
and shredded

1 cup grated
Parmesan cheese

½ cup potato starch

3 eggs

2 teaspoons salt

1 teaspoon garlic powder

Oil, for frying

Sour cream, for garnish

Chopped parsley, for garnish

1 In a large mixing bowl, mix together potatoes, onions and Parmesan cheese. Sprinkle potato starch over the mixture and toss together well.

2 In a small bowl, whisk together eggs, salt and garlic powder. Pour over potato mixture and mix together well.

3 Fill a nonstick skillet with about 1 ½ inches of oil and heat over medium heat. When oil is hot, form patties with ⅓ cup potato mixture and drop them gently into the hot oil. Fry each latke for approximately 3 to 4 minutes per side until golden brown. Repeat until all potato mixture is used.

4 Serve latkes garnished with sour cream and parsley.

**NUTRITION
PER SERVING**
(2 latkes)

Calories: 340

Fat: 26g

Sat Fat: 7g

Cholesterol:
75mg

Sodium:
590mg

Carbs: 18g

Fiber: 2g

Sugars: 2g

Protein: 8g

Creamed Spinach with Garlic & Shallots

Parmesan, cream and just a touch of nutmeg and lemon liven up our nutrient-packed spinach. If your kids are green-shy but love cheese, try this recipe out with some gluten-free fish sticks or grilled salmon.

3 tablespoons butter, divided

2 (9 ounce) bags fresh baby spinach

2 shallots, finely diced

3 cloves garlic, finely minced

¾ cup heavy cream

1 teaspoon nutmeg

1 ½ teaspoons salt

1 ½ cups grated Parmesan cheese

1 teaspoon lemon zest

1 In a large nonstick skillet, heat 2 tablespoons butter over medium-high heat. Add spinach and sauté until wilted, about 4 minutes. Remove spinach from skillet and drain well.

2 In the same skillet, heat remaining tablespoon of butter over medium heat. Add shallots and garlic and cook, stirring often, until softened, about 3 to 4 minutes.

3 Add heavy cream, nutmeg and salt and bring the mixture to a simmer. Cover, reduce heat to medium-low and simmer for 5 to 7 minutes.

4 Stir in Parmesan cheese and lemon zest and continue stirring until cheese has melted and the mixture is smooth. Stir in cooked spinach, cover and heat for an additional 3 to 5 minutes before serving hot.

YIELD
6 servings

PREP TIME
10 minutes

TOTAL TIME
25 minutes

NUTRITION PER SERVING

Calories: 480

Fat: 38g

Sat Fat: 22g

Cholesterol: 115mg

Sodium: 1,920mg

Carbs: 18g

Fiber: 7g

Sugars: 1g

Protein: 22g

YIELD
4 servings

PREP TIME
10 minutes

TOTAL TIME
20 minutes

Green Beans with Tomatoes, Garlic & Onions

Cooking vegetables has never been so simple or so tasty! With just a few simple ingredients, staples like olive oil and salt, green beans and tomatoes go from farm fresh to white tablecloth–ready.

NUTRITION PER SERVING

Calories: 220

Fat: 8g

Sat Fat: 1g

Cholesterol: 0mg

Sodium: 590mg

Carbs: 31g

Fiber: 11g

Sugars: 7g

Protein: 10g

Water, for boiling

1 pound green beans, ends removed

2 tablespoons olive oil

1 large yellow onion, finely chopped

3 cloves garlic, minced

3 large tomatoes, chopped

½ teaspoon red pepper flakes

1 teaspoon salt

1 Heat a large pot of water over high heat. Bring to a boil, set a steamer basket on top and fill with green beans. Steam for 5 to 7 minutes. Remove green beans from steamer and set aside.

2 In a large pot, heat olive oil over medium heat. Add onions and cook, stirring occasionally, until onions are translucent, about 5 minutes. Add garlic and tomatoes and cook, stirring occasionally, until tomatoes are very soft and soupy, about 5 to 7 minutes.

3 Add red pepper flakes and salt and cook 1 additional minute.

4 Toss steamed green beans in with the tomato mixture and cook 2 to 3 minutes. Serve immediately.

Creamy Cheesy Herbed Polenta

This warm side dish made with Gruyère cheese, cream cheese, parsley and basil is a great base for serving with grilled spicy shrimp or alongside a perfectly cooked steak with a tomato-y homemade steak sauce. Though polenta has historically been considered "peasants' food," its creamy and gritty texture makes it a versatile companion for many entrées.

YIELD
4 servings

PREP TIME
10 minutes

TOTAL TIME
25 minutes

2 cups milk

2 ½ cups vegetable stock

1 cup yellow cornmeal

1 teaspoon salt

2 tablespoons butter

1 cup grated Gruyère cheese

½ cup cream cheese

½ cup finely chopped flat leaf parsley

¼ cup finely chopped fresh basil

1 In a medium-sized pot, bring milk and vegetable stock to a boil over medium-high heat. Once liquid comes to a boil, reduce heat to medium-low and vigorously whisk in cornmeal to prevent any lumps from forming. Cook for 8 minutes, stirring frequently.

2 Using a wooden spoon or spatula, stir in salt, butter, Gruyère cheese and cream cheese. Once cheese is fully melted and incorporated, stir in parsley and basil. Serve hot as a side dish.

NUTRITION PER SERVING

Calories: 480

Fat: 29g

Sat Fat: 16g

Cholesterol: 90mg

Sodium: 1,110mg

Carbs: 37g

Fiber: 5g

Sugars: 9g

Protein: 20g

YIELD
24 to 30 bites

PREP TIME
10 minutes

TOTAL TIME
35 minutes

Lemon, Ricotta & Kale Stuffed Mushrooms

All hail kale! Leafy and green kale is one of the most nutritionally complete sources of vitamins A, C and K. Blending kale with lemon, ricotta and honey and just a touch of hot sauce makes these stuffed mushrooms a tasty and wholesome side dish or appetizer.

Foil and nonstick cooking spray, for lining and greasing baking sheet

24 to 30 button mushrooms, stems removed

1 (16 ounce) bag green kale, deribbed and finely chopped

2 shallots, finely minced

1 clove garlic, minced

¼ cup water

1 cup part-skim ricotta cheese

2 teaspoons honey

2 tablespoons lemon juice

Zest of 1 lemon

1 teaspoon salt

¼ teaspoon hot sauce

1 Preheat oven to 400°F. Line a baking sheet with foil and spray lightly with nonstick cooking spray. Arrange mushrooms on prepared baking sheet, stem side down. Roast for 15 minutes. Remove from oven and cool completely.

2 In a large skillet over medium heat, toss together kale, shallots, garlic and water. Cover and steam, stirring occasionally, until kale has wilted and shallots are soft and translucent, about 8 to 10 minutes. Remove from heat and cool completely.

3 Transfer cooled kale mixture to a food processor and add part-skim ricotta, honey, lemon juice, lemon zest, salt and hot sauce. Pulse until a very smooth mixture forms.

4 Spoon heaping portions of kale ricotta filling into each of the roasted mushrooms. Cover and refrigerate until ready to serve.

NUTRITION PER SERVING
(1 bite)

Calories: 30

Fat: 1g

Sat Fat: 0.5g

Cholesterol: 5mg

Sodium: 120mg

Carbs: 4g

Fiber: 1g

Sugars: 1g

Protein: 2g

Three-Cheese Potato Leek Gratin

Both russet and sweet potatoes star in this layered three-cheese gratin. Leeks lend a subtle but sweet flavor to the creamy sauce that makes this side dish shine on any dinner table.

Nonstick cooking spray, to grease casserole dish

4 tablespoons (½ stick) butter

2 cups finely chopped leeks

4 cloves garlic, finely minced

1 tablespoon cornstarch

1 ½ cups whole milk

2 (8 ounce) containers Mascarpone cheese

1 ½ teaspoons nutmeg

2 teaspoons salt

¼ teaspoon pepper

3 russet potatoes, peeled and thinly sliced (about 1 ½ pounds)

3 sweet potatoes, peeled and thinly sliced (about 1 ½ pounds)

2 cups grated Gruyère cheese, divided

2 cups grated white cheddar cheese, divided

1 Preheat oven to 400°F. Grease a 9 x 13-inch casserole dish with nonstick cooking spray and set aside.

2 In a saucepan over medium-low heat, melt butter. Add leeks and cook, stirring occasionally, until leeks are soft, about 5 minutes. Add garlic and cook 1 additional minute.

3 Sprinkle cornstarch over leeks and garlic and toss to coat well.

4 Whisk in milk, Mascarpone cheese, nutmeg, salt and pepper and continue stirring until a smooth sauce forms, about 4 to 5 minutes.

5 Mix potato slices together and divide them into 3 equal portions. Layer ⅓ of potatoes in the bottom of the casserole dish and pour approximately ⅓ of cheese sauce over the potatoes. Sprinkle approximately ⅓ of Gruyère cheese and approximately ⅓ of white cheddar cheese on top of the layer. Repeat process with the remaining 2 layers of potatoes, cheese sauce and grated cheese.

6 Place gratin in the oven and bake for 50 to 55 minutes until potatoes are soft and the mixture is golden brown and bubbly.

YIELD
8 servings

PREP TIME
15 minutes

TOTAL TIME
1 hour
10 minutes

NUTRITION PER SERVING

Calories: 720

Fat: 51g

Sat Fat: 28g

Cholesterol: 150mg

Sodium: 990mg

Carbs: 45g

Fiber: 5g

Sugars: 7g

Protein: 25g

Goat Cheese Fritters with Lemon Honey

Savory fried goat cheese balls with a lemon, honey and red pepper flake dipping sauce are a great side, or you can use the fried goat cheese as a garnish on top of a leafy salad dressed with the lemon honey sauce with basil accents. Goat cheese is soft and characteristically tart. It can sometimes be better tolerated by individuals with a sensitivity to cow's milk.

FOR THE GOAT CHEESE FRITTERS

1 (10.5 ounce) log goat cheese

Parchment paper, for lining baking sheet

¼ cup gluten-free all-purpose flour

1 teaspoon salt

1 egg

1 teaspoon water

1 ½ cups gluten-free bread crumbs

Vegetable oil, for frying

FOR THE LEMON HONEY DIPPING SAUCE

2 tablespoons lemon juice

2 tablespoons honey

Zest of 1 lemon

½ teaspoon salt

¼ teaspoon red pepper flakes

1 To make the goat cheese fritters, cut goat cheese log into 16 evenly sized pieces and then roll each piece into a ball. Place balls on a baking sheet lined with parchment paper and freeze for 20 minutes.

2 Create a breading station with 3 mixing bowls. In 1 bowl, mix together gluten-free all-purpose flour and salt. In the second bowl, whisk together egg and water. In the third bowl, pour in gluten-free bread crumbs.

3 To make the lemon honey dipping sauce, whisk together lemon juice, honey, lemon zest, salt and red pepper flakes. Set aside until ready to serve.

4 In a nonstick skillet, heat about 1 to 2 inches of vegetable oil to 350°F. Remove goat cheese balls from freezer and first roll each ball into the flour mixture, shaking off any excess.

5 Dip each goat cheese ball into egg mixture and then finally into the bread crumbs, being sure to evenly coat each ball.

6 Working in batches, gently drop coated goat cheese balls into the hot oil. Fry each ball for approximately 2 minutes on each side until they are golden brown. Remove fritters from oil using a slotted spoon and drain any excess oil. Repeat until all fritters are fried.

7 Serve goat cheese fritters with lemon honey dipping sauce.

NUTRITION PER SERVING

Calories: 270

Fat: 18g

Sat Fat: 4.5g

Cholesterol: 20mg

Sodium: 290mg

Carbs: 20g

Fiber: 1g

Sugars: 2g

Protein: 6g

YIELD
6 servings

PREP TIME
10 minutes

TOTAL TIME
35 minutes

Apricot Almond Brown Rice Pilaf

This slightly sweet pilaf is made with brown rice, which is higher in fiber and more nutritious than refined white rice. Dried apricots are enlivened by a touch of lemon juice and crunchy slivered almonds.

4 tablespoons extra-virgin olive oil, divided

½ cup finely minced shallots

1 ½ cups long grain brown rice

½ cup chopped slivered almonds, divided

¼ cup dry white wine

1 ¾ cups vegetable stock

½ cup fresh lemon juice

2 tablespoons finely chopped dried apricots

1 teaspoon salt

1 teaspoon lemon zest

Salt, to taste

1 In a large pot, heat 3 tablespoons olive oil over medium heat. Add shallots and cook, stirring frequently, until shallots are transparent, about 3 to 5 minutes.

2 Add remaining tablespoon of olive oil, brown rice and ¼ cup of almonds. Cook, stirring constantly, for about 2 minutes.

3 Add white wine, vegetable stock, lemon juice, apricots and salt. Stir gently, then bring to a boil.

4 Reduce heat to low, cover and cook until all liquid is absorbed and rice is tender, about 22 to 25 minutes.

5 Fluff pilaf with a fork and stir in remaining ¼ cup almonds and lemon zest. Season with salt before serving. Garnish with slivered almonds, if desired.

NUTRITION PER SERVING

Calories: 360

Fat: 16g

Sat Fat: 2g

Cholesterol: 0mg

Sodium: 500mg

Carbs: 46g

Fiber: 3g

Sugars: 5g

Protein: 8g

YIELD
4 servings

PREP TIME
10 minutes

TOTAL TIME
30 minutes

Cheesy Leek Risotto

Despite what you may have heard elsewhere, risotto, an Italian rice dish, can only be made with Arborio rice. This short, stout grain soaks up liquid like a sponge and, once cooked, produces a binding, gelatinous consistency. Dress up this special rice with Parmesan and Gruyère cheese and give it a nutritious bite with crunchy edamame. Serve this dish alongside salmon and a glass of chilled white wine.

4 ½ cups vegetable stock

½ cup dry white wine

1 tablespoon olive oil

2 cups chopped leeks, white and light green parts only

2 cups frozen shelled edamame peas

1 cup Arborio rice

½ cup grated Parmesan cheese

½ cup grated Gruyère cheese

Salt, to taste

Pepper, to taste

1 In a small pot over medium-low heat, combine vegetable stock and white wine. Bring to a slow simmer.

2 In a separate medium-sized pot over medium heat, heat olive oil and then add leeks and edamame peas. Sauté leeks and edamame peas until softened, about 5 to 7 minutes.

3 Add rice to pot with leeks and edamame peas and use a wooden spoon to combine with the vegetables. Cook for 1 minute.

4 Pour 1 cup of warm stock into the pot with rice and vegetables, stir to combine and let cook until liquid is almost fully reduced.

5 Continue this process until all stock mixture has been added to the rice mixture. Keep an eye on heat level so the rice mixture does not scorch and stick to bottom of the pot.

6 Once all liquid has been absorbed, remove pot from the burner and stir in Parmesan and Gruyère cheeses. Stir until well combined and season to taste with salt and pepper. Serve hot as a side dish.

NUTRITION PER SERVING

Calories: 510

Fat: 14g

Sat Fat: 3.5g

Cholesterol: 20mg

Sodium: 860mg

Carbs: 64g

Fiber: 4g

Sugars: 8g

Protein: 28g

PREP TIME
1 hour
15 minutes
(includes
rising time)

TOTAL TIME
1 hour
40 minutes

NUTRITION PER SERVING
(1 flatbread)

Calories: 500

Fat: 26g

Sat Fat: 13g

Cholesterol: 60mg

Sodium: 2,010mg

Carbs: 42g

Fiber: 6g

Sugars: 7g

Protein: 26g

Caramelized Wild Mushrooms & Shallot Flatbreads

Once baked, these filling cheesy flatbreads look like mini mushroom pizzas. The mozzarella and Parmesan cheese cover a sautéed medley of chopped Portobello, button, shiitake and cremini mushrooms, which give this bread a meaty texture. Eat them alone or with a simple grilled protein entrée.

FOR THE CRUST

¾ cup warm water

2 ¼ teaspoons (1 packet) rapid-rise yeast

1 tablespoon olive oil plus additional for oiling the bowl

1 tablespoon sugar

1 ¼ cups gluten-free all-purpose flour plus additional for shaping the flatbreads

1 tablespoon everything spice blend (1 teaspoon dried onion, 1 teaspoon dried garlic, 1 teaspoon poppy seeds)

1 teaspoon sea salt

1 tablespoon apple cider vinegar

Oiled plastic wrap, for covering bowl

FOR THE TOPPING

2 tablespoons butter

1 cup thinly sliced baby Portobello mushrooms

1 cup thinly sliced button mushrooms

1 cup thinly sliced shiitake mushrooms

1 cup thinly sliced cremini mushrooms

2 shallots, finely diced

¼ cup sherry

2 cloves garlic, minced

⅛ cup finely chopped parsley

1 teaspoon salt

Parchment paper, for lining baking sheet

1 cup grated mozzarella cheese

1 cup grated Parmesan cheese

1 To make the crust, in the bowl of a stand mixer using the paddle attachment, combine warm water, yeast, olive oil and sugar and let sit until yeast is puffy, about 5 minutes.

2 In a large bowl, whisk together gluten-free all-purpose flour, everything spice blend and sea salt.

3 Add half of flour mixture to yeast and water mixture and beat on low until well incorporated. Add remaining flour mixture and apple cider vinegar and mix until dough is very sticky and smooth.

4 Place dough in an oiled bowl and cover with oiled plastic wrap. Let rise in a warm place for 45 to 60 minutes.

5 To make the topping, in a large skillet heat butter over medium-high heat. Add mushrooms and shallots and cook, stirring frequently, until the vegetables are golden brown, about 7 to 9 minutes.

6 Deglaze the skillet with sherry and add garlic, parsley and salt. Cook an additional 2 minutes until the liquid has mostly evaporated. Remove from heat and set aside.

7 Preheat oven to 450°F.

8 Turn dough out onto a parchment-lined baking sheet and sprinkle gluten-free all-purpose flour over the top of the dough. Divide dough into 6 evenly sized pieces. Gently stretch and press dough into round crusts. They can be as symmetrical or rustic looking as you would like.

9 Top each flatbread with mushroom and shallot mixture and sprinkle mozzarella and Parmesan cheeses on top. Bake for 10 to 15 minutes until golden. Serve immediately.

YIELD
6 servings

PREP TIME
10 minutes

TOTAL TIME
35 minutes

Lemon Cranberry Pistachio Brown Rice Pilaf

Rice pilafs are incredibly versatile, and lend themselves well to whatever ingredients are in your pantry. The basic recipe is the same, just change up the ingredients to work with whatever you have on hand! This fan favorite version is tangy and sweet, featuring lemon zest, dried cranberries and pistachios.

4 tablespoons extra-virgin olive oil, divided

½ cup finely minced shallots

1 ½ cups extra-long grain brown rice

½ cup chopped pistachios, divided

¼ cup dry white wine

1 ¾ cups vegetable stock

½ cup fresh lemon juice

2 tablespoons finely chopped dried cranberries

1 teaspoon salt

2 tablespoons lemon zest

Salt, to taste

1 In a large pot, heat 3 tablespoons of olive oil over medium heat. Add shallots and cook, stirring frequently, until shallots are transparent, about 3 to 5 minutes.

2 Add remaining tablespoon of olive oil, brown rice and ¼ cup of pistachios. Cook, stirring constantly, for about 2 minutes.

3 Add white wine, vegetable stock, lemon juice, cranberries and salt. Stir gently, then bring to a boil.

4 Reduce heat to low, cover and cook until all liquid is absorbed and the rice is tender, about 22 to 25 minutes.

5 Fluff pilaf with a fork and stir in remaining ¼ cup pistachios and lemon zest. Season with salt before serving. Garnish with chopped cranberries, if desired.

NUTRITION PER SERVING

Calories: 370

Fat: 16g

Sat Fat: 2.5g

Cholesterol: 0mg

Sodium: 490mg

Carbs: 48g

Fiber: 3g

Sugars: 6g

Protein: 8g

Spicy Orange Sesame Carrots

Adding ginger, garlic and a few other Asian flavors gives a fresh take on the classic side dish of carrots cooked in orange juice. (See photo on pages 120–121.)

(See photo on pages 120–121.)

3 cups thinly sliced carrots (slice on the diagonal)

¼ cup water

¼ cup freshly squeezed orange juice

¼ cup chopped green onions

1 teaspoon gluten-free, reduced-sodium soy sauce

1 teaspoon toasted sesame oil

1 teaspoon rice vinegar

1 teaspoon grated ginger

1 teaspoon minced garlic

¾ teaspoon toasted sesame seeds

½ teaspoon grated orange zest

¼ teaspoon red pepper flakes

1 Place carrots into a saucepan. Add water, cover and cook over medium-low heat for 8 to 10 minutes.

2 In a small bowl, whisk together orange juice, green onions, gluten-free soy sauce, sesame oil, rice vinegar, ginger, garlic, sesame seeds, orange zest and red pepper flakes. Mix well and set aside.

3 Remove cover from carrots, stir and cook another 5 minutes until the water has entirely evaporated.

4 Pour orange juice mixture over the carrots and cook an additional 5 minutes uncovered. Remove from heat and serve warm.

YIELD
4 servings

PREP TIME
15 minutes

TOTAL TIME
40 minutes

NUTRITION PER SERVING

Calories: 70

Fat: 2g

Sat Fat: 0g

Cholesterol: 0mg

Sodium: 150mg

Carbs: 12g

Fiber: 3g

Sugars: 6g

Protein: 1g

Sweet Potato, Apple & Brie Gratin

YIELD
4 servings

PREP TIME
15 minutes

TOTAL TIME
1 hour
15 minutes

This spiraled gratin made with sweet potatoes and Granny Smith apples covered in melted Brie is a beautiful side dish worthy of the holidays. Brie is a soft cow's milk cheese with a mild and sweet flavor that is high in protein and both vitamins B_{12} and B_2.

Nonstick cooking spray, to grease pie pan or glass baking dish

1 large sweet potato (or 2 smaller potatoes), peeled and sliced into thin rounds

2 large Granny Smith apples, sliced into thin rounds

½ cup brown sugar

⅓ cup golden raisins

8 ounces Brie cheese, rind removed

½ cup cream

Foil, for covering the baking dish

1 Preheat oven to 375°F. Lightly grease a round pie pan or glass baking dish with nonstick cooking spray and set aside.

2 In the baking dish, create layers of sweet potatoes and apples. Alternate sweet potatoes and apples in an even layer. Repeat, creating a spiral until all sweet potatoes and apples are used and the spiral ends.

3 Sprinkle brown sugar evenly over the gratin. Add raisins in an even layer on top of the sugar.

4 Cut Brie into small pieces, about 1-inch pats, and place them over the gratin until covered. Pour cream evenly over top of the gratin.

5 Cover with foil and bake for 40 to 45 minutes until cream is bubbly. Remove foil and bake until cheese is slightly browned. Let cool for at least 10 minutes before slicing. Serve as a side dish.

NUTRITION PER SERVING

Calories: 560

Fat: 27g

Sat Fat: 17g

Cholesterol: 100mg

Sodium: 340mg

Carbs: 69g

Fiber: 5g

Sugars: 50g

Protein: 14g

YIELD
4 servings

PREP TIME
15 minutes

TOTAL TIME
35 minutes

Red Wine Glazed Mushroom Rosemary Skewers

Mushrooms take on a meatiness when marinated and cooked in this red wine sauce. The rosemary sprigs add another depth of flavor and give the dish a high-class look when plated.

1 (0.66 ounce) package fresh rosemary

1 pound whole cremini mushrooms, stems removed

1 ½ cups Cabernet Sauvignon wine

1 small bay leaf

1 clove garlic, finely minced

1 tablespoon finely diced shallots

8 whole peppercorns

4 sprigs fresh thyme

2 tablespoons unsalted butter

⅛ teaspoon salt

Nonstick cooking spray, to grease skillet

1 Using the wooden bottom of a rosemary sprig, gently pierce through the middle of the gill side of a mushroom. Continue until 3 to 5 mushrooms are on the sprig. Repeat until all mushrooms have been skewered.

2 Place mushrooms in a 9 x 13-inch baking dish and set aside.

3 In a saucepan, combine Cabernet Sauvignon, bay leaf, garlic, shallots, peppercorns, thyme, butter and salt. Cook over medium heat for approximately 10 minutes, until liquid has reduced by about half.

4 Remove mixture from heat and pour through a strainer over the mushroom skewers. Discard solids from the strainer.

5 Cover mushrooms and let sit on the counter for 20 minutes, rotating the skewers halfway through.

6 Heat a skillet over medium-high heat and lightly coat the skillet with nonstick cooking spray. Add 2 to 3 skewers of mushrooms to the skillet at a time. Do not overcrowd.

7 Sear mushrooms in the skillet for about 1 minute, turning once to get an even sear. Transfer skewers to a serving plate. Repeat until all skewers are cooked.

8 Add remaining wine mixture to the skillet, warm through and pour over the mushrooms. Serve immediately.

NUTRITION PER SERVING

Calories: 160

Fat: 6g

Sat Fat: 4g

Cholesterol: 15mg

Sodium: 80mg

Carbs: 9g

Fiber: 2g

Sugars: 2g

Protein: 3g

YIELD
6 servings

PREP TIME
10 minutes

TOTAL TIME
15 minutes

Orange Zest Steamed Vegetables

Farm-fresh vegetables are simply steamed with natural orange zest and juice. It doesn't get any more simply delicious! This side dish is perfect for those busy weeknights when there's just no time for a lavish meal.

NUTRITION PER SERVING

Calories: 130

Fat: 5g

Sat Fat: 0.5g

Cholesterol: 0mg

Sodium: 470mg

Carbs: 19g

Fiber: 7g

Sugars: 8g

Protein: 6g

1 head broccoli, ends trimmed and cut into bite-sized pieces

1 head cauliflower, ends trimmed and cut into bite-sized pieces

5 carrots, peeled and cut into bite-sized pieces

2 tablespoons olive oil

Zest of 1 orange

Plastic wrap, for covering bowl

Juice of 1 orange

1 teaspoon salt

1 In a large microwave-safe bowl, toss together broccoli, cauliflower, carrots, olive oil and orange zest. Cover with plastic wrap and microwave on high for 4 to 5 minutes until vegetables are soft.

2 Remove from microwave and drain excess liquid. Toss vegetables with orange juice and salt before serving.

Garlic Parmesan Shoestring French Fries

Loved by kids and approved by adults, too! These skinny fries are seasoned with a subtle spice mixture that's basic enough for the little ones, yet complex enough for any dinner party.

3 tablespoons extra-virgin olive oil, divided

Foil, for lining baking sheet

2 russet potatoes, peeled

1 teaspoon garlic powder

1 teaspoon dried parsley

1 teaspoon coarse salt

1 cup grated Parmesan cheese

1 Preheat oven to 425°F. Drizzle 1 tablespoon olive oil across the surface of 2 baking sheets lined with foil and set aside.

2 Using a mandolin, slice potatoes into thin pieces. Set pieces on top of each other to make a stack and, using a sharp knife, cut the potatoes into long thin strips.

3 In a large bowl, toss potato strips with remaining 2 tablespoons olive oil. Toss potatoes with garlic powder, parsley and salt. Spread potatoes out on prepared baking sheet in a single layer.

4 Cook for 20 to 30 minutes, turning occasionally with a metal spatula until the potatoes are golden brown and crisp. Base your cook time on the level of crispiness desired.

5 Sprinkle Parmesan cheese on top of fries and put them back into the oven for 1 to 2 minutes until cheese is melted.

6 Serve garlic Parmesan shoestring French fries with ketchup or another dipping sauce.

YIELD
4 servings

PREP TIME
25 minutes

TOTAL TIME
35 to 40 minutes

NUTRITION PER SERVING

Calories: 330

Fat: 22g

Sat Fat: 6g

Cholesterol: 20mg

Sodium: 1,080mg

Carbs: 20g

Fiber: 2g

Sugars: 1g

Protein: 14g

Curry Coconut Mashed Cauliflower

YIELD
4 servings

PREP TIME
5 minutes

TOTAL TIME
15 minutes

Can't decide between Thai food and good old-fashioned mashed potatoes? This recipe for mashed cauliflower is packed with genuine Thai flavors and cuts down dramatically on the fat and calories of traditional mashed potatoes. If you're unfamiliar with coconut cream, it's the creamy part when you open a can of coconut milk. Simply scoop off 2 tablespoons for this recipe.

Water, for boiling

1 large head cauliflower, ends trimmed and chopped into small pieces

2 tablespoons coconut cream

1 tablespoon red curry paste

2 cloves garlic, peeled

½ teaspoon salt

1 Prepare a steamer basket over a pot of boiling water. Steam cauliflower for 8 to 10 minutes until soft. Drain cauliflower and pat dry with paper towels.

2 Transfer cauliflower to a food processor and add coconut cream, red curry paste, garlic and salt. Purée until a nearly smooth mixture forms. Garnish with chopped scallions, if desired. Serve immediately.

NUTRITION PER SERVING

Calories: 70

Fat: 3g

Sat Fat: 2.5g

Cholesterol: 0mg

Sodium: 320mg

Carbs: 10g

Fiber: 5g

Sugars: 4g

Protein: 4g

CHAPTER SIX

Main Dishes

Spiced Bourbon Carnitas Tacos – page 168

Marinated Flank Steak & Zucchini Arepas with Peach Guacamole

YIELD
6 servings

PREP TIME
20 minutes

TOTAL TIME
55 minutes

Arepas are corn cakes made from masa harina, or finely ground cornmeal. The smokiness and spice of the cumin and paprika in the arepas complement the citrus marinade on the flank steak. Add a dollop of sweet and tangy peach guacamole to round out this South American–style dish.

FOR THE MARINADE

¼ cup orange juice

¼ cup lime juice

1 peach, pitted and roughly chopped

½ cup fresh cilantro leaves

¼ cup diced red onion

2 cloves garlic

2 tablespoons brown sugar

2 tablespoons olive oil

1 teaspoon ground cumin

½ teaspoon chili powder

1 teaspoon salt

FOR THE FLANK STEAK AND ZUCCHINI

2 pounds flank steak, thinly sliced

1 pound zucchini, thinly sliced

FOR THE AREPAS

2 cups masa harina (finely ground cornmeal)

2 teaspoons smoked paprika

1 teaspoon ground cumin

¾ teaspoon salt

½ teaspoon onion powder

½ teaspoon garlic powder

1 ¾ cups hot water

Canola oil, for frying

FOR THE PEACH GUACAMOLE

2 ripe avocados, peeled and seeds removed

½ cup finely chopped fresh cilantro leaves

2 tablespoons lime juice

½ teaspoon salt

1 peach, pitted and finely diced

1 To make the marinade, in a blender, purée together orange juice, lime juice, peaches, cilantro, red onion, garlic, brown sugar, olive oil, cumin, chili powder and salt until a smooth liquid forms.

2 To make the flank steak and zucchini, place sliced steak and zucchini in a large bowl, pour the marinade over the top and toss together to fully coat all pieces of steak and zucchini. Cover and refrigerate for 30 minutes.

3 To make the arepas, in a large mixing bowl, whisk together masa harina, smoked paprika, cumin, salt, onion powder and garlic powder. Add hot water and mix well.

4 Form dough into a ball and then divide into 6 equally sized pieces. Press each piece of dough into a patty that is about 1 inch thick.

5 Heat a heavy-bottomed skillet over medium heat. Add just enough canola oil to coat bottom of the pan. Cook the arepas patties in batches, about 4 to 6 minutes per side until golden brown. Set aside until ready to serve.

6 To make the peach guacamole, mash together avocados, cilantro, lime juice and salt. Fold in peaches. Cover and refrigerate until ready to serve.

7 To cook the flank steak and zucchini, preheat a heavy-bottomed skillet over high heat. Drain marinade off the steak and zucchini and add to the heated skillet. Cook for 3 to 4 minutes per side until seared and golden.

8 To serve, place an arepa on each plate. Place a heaping portion of flank steak and zucchini on top of each arepa and top with a dollop of peach guacamole. Serve immediately.

NUTRITION PER SERVING

Calories: 960

Fat: 65g

Sat Fat: 9g

Cholesterol: 120mg

Sodium: 980mg

Carbs: 50g

Fiber: 9g

Sugars: 12g

Protein: 49g

YIELD
4 servings

PREP TIME
10 minutes

TOTAL TIME
30 minutes

Sautéed Shrimp & Broccoli with Penne Pasta & Lemon Mascarpone Cream Sauce

This Italian-style dish is easy to make, with a sweet and creamy sauce. Mascarpone—while most often is used in tiramisu—adds a layer of richness to the lemony shrimp.

Water, for boiling

1 (12 ounce) package gluten-free corn penne pasta

1 (12 ounce) bag frozen broccoli florets

1 tablespoon olive oil

1 ¼ pounds shrimp, peeled and deveined

2 shallots, finely minced

3 cloves garlic, finely minced

½ cup white wine

¾ cup chicken stock

½ cup lemon juice

1 (8 ounce) container Mascarpone cheese

2 teaspoons lemon zest

1 teaspoon salt

Freshly grated Parmesan cheese, for garnish

1 Fill a large pot with water and bring to a boil over high heat. Add gluten-free penne pasta and cook for 10 minutes, stirring occasionally. Add broccoli florets and cook an additional 2 minutes. Drain pasta and broccoli under cold water and set aside.

2 In a large high-sided skillet, heat olive oil over medium-high heat. Add shrimp and cook, stirring occasionally, until the shrimp start turning pink. Add shallots and garlic and cook 2 to 3 minutes, stirring frequently.

3 Add white wine to deglaze skillet and simmer until most of the liquid has evaporated. Add chicken stock and lemon juice and bring to a rolling boil.

4 Reduce heat to medium and stir in Mascarpone cheese, lemon zest and salt. Simmer, stirring constantly, for 3 to 4 minutes.

5 Toss gluten-free penne and broccoli into the shrimp mixture and stir to coat well. Divide mixture into serving bowls and garnish with grated Parmesan cheese. Serve immediately.

NUTRITION PER SERVING

Calories: 670

Fat: 33g

Sat Fat: 15g

Cholesterol: 95mg

Sodium: 850mg

Carbs: 75g

Fiber: 10g

Sugars: 3g

Protein: 15g

YIELD
5 servings
(2 crepes per
serving)

PREP TIME
35 minutes

TOTAL TIME
45 minutes

Savory Crepes with Fresh Mozzarella, Salami & Avocado

Though French crepes are typically made with wheat flour, these gluten-free ones are made with buckwheat flour and cornstarch. Cooked in a pan the way you might a pancake, these light and thin crepes are the perfect base for any number of filling combinations, from mushrooms and caramelized onions to Nutella with chunks of banana or ricotta cheese with powdered sugar.

5 tablespoons butter, melted

1 cup buckwheat flour

2 tablespoons cornstarch

2 cups milk

3 eggs

½ teaspoon salt

Nonstick cooking spray, for greasing skillet

2 cups grated mozzarella cheese

20 slices salami

2 avocados, peeled, seeds removed and each thinly sliced into 10 pieces

1 In a blender or food processor, combine melted butter, buckwheat flour, cornstarch, milk, eggs and salt. Purée until a smooth batter forms. Cover and refrigerate for 30 minutes.

2 Heat an 8-inch nonstick skillet over medium heat and spray with nonstick cooking spray. Pour ⅓ cup of batter into the skillet and cook for about 2 minutes until the crepe sets and edges begin to brown. Carefully flip crepe over and cook an additional 2 minutes.

3 Sprinkle mozzarella cheese across surface of the crepe and then layer 2 pieces of salami and 2 pieces of avocado on top of the cheese. When cheese begins to melt, roll the crepe. Remove from skillet and set aside. Repeat with the remaining batter to make 10 complete crepes. Be sure to spray the skillet with nonstick cooking spray before each addition of batter. Serve immediately.

NUTRITION PER SERVING
(2 crepes)

Calories: 270

Fat: 19g

Sat Fat: 9g

Cholesterol: 105mg

Sodium: 520mg

Carbs: 15g

Fiber: 3g

Sugars: 3g

Protein: 12g

Grilled Salmon with Papaya Gremolata

Deliciously soft and sweet, papaya adds a tropical flavor to this untraditional gremolata. Scoop heaping portions on top of the omega-3 rich salmon for a meal packed with a slew of essential vitamins and minerals.

YIELD
4 servings

PREP TIME
15 minutes

TOTAL TIME
30 minutes

FOR THE PAPAYA GREMOLATA

1 cup very finely chopped papaya

2 cloves garlic, finely minced

Zest of 1 lime

Juice of 1 lime

¼ cup finely minced parsley

2 tablespoons extra-virgin olive oil

½ teaspoon salt

FOR THE SALMON

Vegetable oil, for greasing grill

¼ cup honey or agave nectar

2 tablespoons lemon juice

1 teaspoon salt

1 teaspoon garlic powder

½ teaspoon pepper

4 salmon steaks (approximately 5 ounces each)

1 To make the papaya gremolata, in a mixing bowl, mix together papaya, garlic, lime zest, lime juice and parsley. Drizzle mixture with olive oil and salt and gently mix together. Cover and refrigerate until ready to serve.

2 To make the salmon, preheat grill over medium-high heat and brush the grill with vegetable oil to prevent the fish from sticking.

3 In a small bowl, whisk together honey or agave nectar, lemon juice, salt, garlic powder and pepper. Brush mixture evenly over both sides of each piece of salmon.

4 Grill salmon steaks for approximately 5 minutes per side until salmon flakes easily and reaches an internal temperature of 130°F.

5 Serve grilled salmon topped with chilled papaya gremolata.

NUTRITION PER SERVING

Calories: 860

Fat: 80g

Sat Fat: 10g

Cholesterol: 85mg

Sodium: 950mg

Carbs: 14g

Fiber: 1g

Sugars: 11g

Protein: 29g

YIELD
6 servings

PREP TIME
10 minutes

TOTAL TIME
35 minutes

⊛ Black Bean, Mushroom & Pesto Veggie Burgers

Herbal notes of basil pesto with slightly salty and sweet Gruyère cheese liven up these protein-rich black bean and mushroom veggie burgers. Garnish them with honey mustard, sliced avocado and sun-dried tomatoes with a side of sweet potato fries for a meal sure to please even the most discerning meat-eater's palate.

Parchment paper, for lining baking sheet

1 (15 ounce) can black beans, drained

1 pound Portobello mushrooms

4 cups cooked brown rice, cooled

½ cup pesto sauce

1 cup shredded Gruyère cheese

1 egg

1 teaspoon salt

½ teaspoon garlic powder

6 gluten-free hamburger buns (store-bought or see recipe on page 64)

Optional garnishes: honey mustard, sliced avocado and sun-dried tomatoes

1 Preheat oven to 375°F. Line a baking sheet with parchment paper and set aside.

2 In the bowl of a food processor, combine black beans and mushrooms. Pulse 4 to 5 times just until broken up. Add brown rice, pesto sauce, cheese, egg, salt and garlic powder and pulse until coarse crumbs form.

3 Form mixture into 6 equally sized patties, about ½ cup each and place onto prepared baking sheet. Bake for 20 to 25 minutes until fully set.

4 Serve patties on gluten-free buns with desired garnishes.

NUTRITION PER SERVING

Calories: 820

Fat: 41g

Sat Fat: 8g

Cholesterol: 60mg

Sodium: 770mg

Carbs: 96g

Fiber: 7g

Sugars: 3g

Protein: 16g

Chicken Salad Summer Rolls
with Peach & Radish Salad

YIELD
4 servings
(2 rolls per serving)

PREP TIME
15 minutes

TOTAL TIME
30 minutes

Summertime is a bountiful time for fresh fruits and vegetables. This recipe takes advantage of the best of the season: sweet peaches, mellow avocados, juicy cucumbers and vibrant radishes. The light chicken salad rolled in thin rice paper with slices of avocado and cucumber is refreshing alongside the simple peach and radish salad.

FOR THE SUMMER ROLLS

4 cups cooked rotisserie chicken, diced into small pieces

2 large peaches, pitted and finely diced

1 small shallot, finely diced

¼ cup cilantro leaves, finely chopped

3 tablespoons mayonnaise

1 teaspoon garlic powder

½ teaspoon salt

2 avocados, seeds removed and thinly sliced

1 cucumber, ends removed and thinly sliced into 3-inch strips

8 rice paper wrappers

FOR THE PEACH AND RADISH SALAD

4 large peaches, pitted and diced

2 large radishes, thinly diced

¼ cup cilantro leaves, finely chopped

2 tablespoons extra-virgin olive oil

½ tablespoon honey

2 teaspoons red wine vinegar

½ teaspoon salt

1 To make the summer rolls, in a mixing bowl, mix together chicken, peaches, shallots, cilantro, mayonnaise, garlic powder and salt. Mix well and set aside.

2 Set up a rolling station with the bowl of chicken salad and the avocados and cucumbers.

3 Run rice paper wrappers under cool water until soft, according to package instructions. Scoop a heaping portion of chicken salad into each wrapper and place 2 slices of avocado and 2 slices of cucumber on top. Wrap rolls up just as you would a burrito, folding in the sides first and then rolling it up tightly lengthwise. Repeat with each of the 8 rolls.

4 To make the peach and radish salad, in a mixing bowl, toss together peaches, radishes and cilantro. In a separate bowl, whisk together olive oil, honey, red wine vinegar and salt. Pour dressing over the salad and toss well. Serve salad with the summer rolls.

NUTRITION PER SERVING
(2 rolls)

Calories: 720

Fat: 32g

Sat Fat: 5g

Cholesterol: 120mg

Sodium: 790mg

Carbs: 63g

Fiber: 13g

Sugars: 32g

Protein: 52g

YIELD
8 servings

PREP TIME
15 minutes

TOTAL TIME
45 minutes

Creamy Macaroni & Cheese with Turkey Sausage & Mushrooms

Finally, a grown-up macaroni and cheese that even the kids will enjoy. Delightfully garlicky and cheesy with hearty turkey sausage and button mushrooms, this soul-warming mac and cheese is covered with a satisfyingly crunchy pretzel topping. Serve it with a gluten-free beer for the adults and a root beer for the kids.

FOR THE PASTA

Water, for boiling

1 pound gluten-free elbow pasta

2 tablespoons olive oil

1 ¼ pounds turkey sausage, casings removed

1 pound thinly sliced button mushrooms

6 tablespoons butter

½ cup cornstarch

4 ½ cups warm milk

3 cups grated sharp cheddar cheese

3 cups grated Gruyère cheese

2 teaspoons garlic powder

2 teaspoons nutmeg

2 teaspoons sea salt

FOR THE TOPPING

1 ½ cups crushed gluten-free pretzels

½ cup grated Gruyère cheese

2 teaspoons garlic powder

¼ teaspoon salt

2 tablespoons butter, melted

1 Preheat oven to 350°F.

2 To make the pasta, in a large pot, cook gluten-free pasta according to package instructions. Drain and set aside.

3 In a sauté pan, heat olive oil over medium-high heat. Add turkey sausage and cook, stirring frequently, until the sausage is broken up into tiny pieces. Add mushrooms and cook, stirring occasionally, until the sausage and mushrooms are golden brown, about 7 to 9 minutes. Remove from heat and set aside.

4 In a medium-sized saucepan, heat butter over medium-high heat. Whisk in cornstarch until smooth. Cook, whisking constantly, for 3 minutes. Whisk in warm milk and continue stirring until a thick sauce forms, about 3 to 5 minutes.

5 Remove milk mixture from heat and whisk in cheddar cheese and Gruyère cheese. Continue stirring until smooth. Stir in garlic powder, nutmeg and sea salt.

6 In a large mixing bowl, stir together cooked pasta, turkey sausage and mushroom mixture and cheese sauce. Pour mixture into 8 individual gratin dishes or a 9 x 13-inch glass baking dish.

7 To make the topping, mix together gluten-free pretzels, Gruyère cheese, garlic powder, salt and melted butter. Sprinkle mixture on top of macaroni and cheese and bake for 25 to 30 minutes until golden and bubbly. Serve immediately.

NUTRITION PER SERVING

Calories: 1,110

Fat: 63g

Sat Fat: 27g

Cholesterol: 180mg

Sodium: 1,730mg

Carbs: 93g

Fiber: 6g

Sugars: 10g

Protein: 48g

YIELD
4 servings

PREP TIME
10 minutes

TOTAL TIME
35 minutes

Pan-Seared Chicken Cutlets with Mushroom Gravy

With such a lean protein like chicken, it's okay to ladle on a little gravy. Using the pan drippings from the lightly seasoned chicken breasts, you can whip up the creamy gravy you've been missing. The rest, as they say, is gravy.

2 cups white rice

FOR THE CHICKEN

4 boneless, skinless chicken breasts

Plastic wrap for flattening chicken

2 teaspoons salt plus additional to season

1 teaspoon pepper

3 tablespoons butter, divided

Foil, for covering chicken

FOR THE MUSHROOM GRAVY

1 pound thinly sliced button mushrooms

½ cup finely diced yellow onion

2 cloves garlic, minced

½ cup white wine

2 teaspoons cornstarch

½ cup warm chicken stock

¼ cup heavy cream

¼ cup finely chopped flat leaf parsley

1 Cook white rice in a rice cooker or on the stove according to package instructions. Set aside until ready to serve with chicken.

2 To make the chicken, place each breast between 2 pieces of plastic wrap and using a mallet, gently pound until the chicken is approximately a ½ inch thick. Sprinkle both sides of each breast with salt and pepper.

3 In a large sauté pan, heat 2 tablespoons butter over medium-high heat. Add chicken breasts and cook approximately 5 to 7 minutes on each side until the chicken is golden brown and reaches an internal temperature of 165°F.

4 Remove chicken breasts from the pan and cover with foil to keep warm.

5 To make the mushroom gravy, using the same pan with chicken drippings, add remaining 1 tablespoon of butter and heat over medium-high heat. Add mushrooms and onions and cook, stirring frequently until golden brown, about 5 to 7 minutes. Add garlic and cook 1 additional minute.

6 Add white wine to deglaze the pan. Cook, stirring frequently, until the wine has reduced by about half.

7 Whisk together cornstarch and chicken stock and add to the pan. Bring to a simmer and cook until the liquid reduces by half. Add heavy cream, bring back to a simmer and cook for 3 to 5 minutes until sauce is thick enough to coat the back of a spoon. Stir in parsley and season to taste with salt.

8 Serve chicken breasts on top of cooked white rice and top with a generous portion of the mushroom gravy.

NUTRITION PER SERVING

Calories: 470

Fat: 18g

Sat Fat: 10g

Cholesterol: 115mg

Sodium: 680mg

Carbs: 38g

Fiber: 2g

Sugars: 4g

Protein: 33g

Honey BBQ Sloppy Joes with Apple Cabbage Avocado Slaw

YIELD
4 servings

PREP TIME
10 minutes

TOTAL TIME
25 minutes

Sloppy Joes are a classic American sandwich made from ground beef smothered in a spicey tomato sauce. Our variation sweetens the deal and tops the sandwich with a slightly acidic but fresh slaw that takes it into the land of barbecue. All that's missing is the red-checkered picnic tablecloth!

FOR THE HONEY BBQ SLOPPY JOES

2 tablespoons olive oil

1 cup finely diced white onion

3 cloves garlic, minced

1 pound ground chicken

1 (8 ounce) can tomato sauce

½ cup chicken stock

2 tablespoons honey

2 tablespoons brown sugar

2 tablespoons Worcestershire sauce

1 teaspoon paprika

2 teaspoons salt

½ teaspoon crushed red pepper flakes

6 gluten-free ciabatta rolls

FOR THE APPLE CABBAGE AVOCADO SLAW

1 head green cabbage, shredded

1 cup shredded carrots

1 cup shredded red apple

¼ cup golden raisins

¾ cup mayonnaise

¼ cup sour cream

2 tablespoons sugar

2 tablespoons apple cider vinegar

1 teaspoon dry mustard

1 teaspoon salt

1 avocado, peeled, seed removed and diced

1 To make the honey BBQ Sloppy Joes, in a large skillet, heat olive oil over medium-high heat. Add onions and cook, stirring occasionally, until onions are translucent, about 5 minutes. Add garlic and cook 1 additional minute until fragrant.

2 Add ground chicken and cook, stirring occasionally, until browned, about 5 to 7 minutes.

3 Add tomato sauce, chicken stock, honey, brown sugar, Worcestershire sauce, paprika, salt and red pepper flakes and cook, stirring occasionally, until mixture thickens, about 5 minutes. Reduce heat to low.

4 To make the apple cabbage avocado slaw, in a mixing bowl, toss together cabbage, carrots, apples and raisins. In a separate small bowl, whisk together mayonnaise, sour cream, sugar, apple cider vinegar, dry mustard and salt. Pour dressing over the slaw and toss together well. Gently add avocado.

5 Toast gluten-free rolls and place a heaping portion of the honey BBQ Sloppy Joes mixture onto each roll. Serve with a side of apple cabbage avocado slaw.

NUTRITION PER SERVING

Calories: 1,080

Fat: 49g

Sat Fat: 9g

Cholesterol: 115mg

Sodium: 2,030mg

Carbs: 132g

Fiber: 20g

Sugars: 59g

Protein: 36g

Sausage-Stuffed Portobello Mushrooms

 FAN FAVORITE

Portobello mushroom caps are large and thick with a meaty texture. Once stuffed with a tangy but sweet mix of Italian sausage, tomatoes, brown sugar, red wine vinegar and mozzarella cheese, you can eat them with your hands just like a slice of pizza. In fact, you can even experiment with this recipe by adding your favorite pizza toppings and making a personal Portobello pizza!

YIELD
4 servings

PREP TIME
15 minutes

TOTAL TIME
40 minutes

FOR THE PORTOBELLO MUSHROOMS

Foil and nonstick cooking spray, for lining and greasing the baking sheet

4 large Portobello mushroom caps, stems removed

Sea salt

FOR THE STUFFING

2 teaspoons olive oil

1 pound sweet Italian sausage, casings removed

1 large sweet yellow onion, finely diced

2 cloves garlic, finely minced

½ teaspoon oregano

1 (14.5 ounce) can crushed tomatoes, drained

2 tablespoons brown sugar

1 tablespoon red wine vinegar

1 teaspoon salt

1 ½ cups shredded mozzarella cheese

1 Preheat oven to 425°F. Line a baking sheet with foil and spray with nonstick cooking spray and set aside.

2 To make the portobello mushrooms, place mushrooms on prepared baking sheet, stem side up. Sprinkle each mushroom cap lightly with sea salt. Bake for 10 minutes, then remove from oven and drain off any liquids.

3 To make the stuffing, heat olive oil in a large skillet over medium-high heat. Add sausage and, using a spoon, break it up into very small pieces. Once sausage is starting to brown, add onions. Cook, stirring frequently, until onions are translucent, about 7 minutes.

4 Add garlic, oregano, tomatoes, brown sugar, red wine vinegar and salt. Cook, stirring frequently, for 3 to 4 minutes until very fragrant. Remove from heat and set aside for 5 minutes to cool slightly.

5 Toss mozzarella cheese with cooled sausage mixture and then evenly distribute the mixture among the 4 mushroom caps. Bake for 15 to 20 minutes until cheese is golden brown. Serve immediately.

NUTRITION PER SERVING

Calories: 400

Fat: 23g

Sat Fat: 12g

Cholesterol: 70mg

Sodium: 2,330mg

Carbs: 20g

Fiber: 2g

Sugars: 11g

Protein: 32g

YIELD
8 crab cakes

PREP TIME
30 minutes

TOTAL TIME
45 minutes

Mango Crab Cakes with Cilantro Lime Dipping Sauce

Crab—a delicacy usually reserved for special evenings out on the town—can now be on the menu for your next night in. The playful tango of mango, cilantro and citrus take the traditional crab cake to a whole new (and gently spicy) level. Serve it with the sour cream and avocado–based dipping sauce and a margarita to really get your fiesta going.

FOR THE CILANTRO LIME DIPPING SAUCE

¾ cup sour cream

1 avocado, peeled and seed removed

¼ cup freshly chopped cilantro leaves

2 ½ tablespoons lime juice

1 teaspoon sugar

½ teaspoon salt

½ teaspoon hot sauce

½ teaspoon cumin

FOR THE CRAB CAKES

1 pound finely chopped fresh jumbo lump crabmeat

1 cup finely diced mango

2 large eggs, lightly beaten

½ cup cornstarch

¼ cup mayonnaise

¼ cup chopped shallots

½ cup finely chopped fresh cilantro leaves

1 tablespoon fresh lemon juice

1 ½ teaspoons Worcestershire sauce

1 teaspoon cumin

1 teaspoon dry mustard

2 to 3 dashes hot sauce

1 teaspoon salt

Plastic wrap, for covering bowl

Nonstick cooking spray, for greasing baking sheet

1 To make the cilantro lime dipping sauce, in a food processor, combine all the ingredients for the sauce. Pulse until smooth. Transfer to a bowl, cover and refrigerate until ready to serve.

2 To make the crab cakes, in a large mixing bowl, combine crabmeat, mango, eggs, cornstarch, mayonnaise, shallots, cilantro, lemon juice, Worcestershire sauce, cumin, dry mustard, hot sauce and salt. Mix together well until all ingredients are fully incorporated. Cover with plastic wrap and chill in the refrigerator for 20 minutes.

3 Preheat oven to 375°F. Spray a baking sheet with non-stick cooking spray.

4 Divide crab mixture into ⅓ cup–sized patties, using a measuring cup and your hands to form the round cakes.

5 Place formed cakes on prepared baking sheet and bake for 15 to 18 minutes until lightly golden.

6 Serve crab cakes with cilantro lime dipping sauce.

NUTRITION PER SERVING

Calories: 470

Fat: 40g

Sat Fat: 8g

Cholesterol: 100mg

Sodium: 580mg

Carbs: 18g

Fiber: 3g

Sugars: 4g

Protein: 14g

YIELD
6 servings
(3 tacos per
serving)

PREP TIME
15 minutes

TOTAL TIME
4 hours
30 minutes
to 5 hours

Beer Braised Brisket Tacos

Brisket is a thick and strong cut of beef that requires a low and slow cooking method. Try these tender and juicy braised tacos cooked in a tangy beer marinade topped with a tart green tomatillo and cilantro salsa.

FOR THE BRISKET TACOS

3 pound beef brisket,
cut into 3 equal pieces

2 cups sliced yellow onion

1 ½ cups tomato sauce

1 ½ cups gluten-free lager beer

1 cup brown sugar

½ cup gluten-free soy sauce

¼ cup cider vinegar

¼ cup Worcestershire sauce

2 teaspoons ground cumin

½ teaspoon chili powder

Foil, for covering brisket

18 corn tortillas

FOR THE TOMATILLO AND CILANTRO SALSA

1 cup finely diced tomatillos

½ cup finely diced white onion

½ cup finely minced cilantro

1 tablespoon lime juice

¼ teaspoon salt

1 avocado, peeled, seed
removed and diced

1 Preheat oven to 350°F.

2 To make the brisket tacos, place brisket in a large roasting pan or casserole dish. Arrange onions on top and around the brisket.

3 In a mixing bowl, whisk together tomato sauce, gluten-free beer, brown sugar, gluten-free soy sauce, cider vinegar, Worcestershire sauce, cumin and chili powder. Pour sauce over the brisket. Cover brisket with foil and cook 3 hours. Remove foil and cook additional 1 to 1 ½ hours until brisket is fork tender and easily pulls away into shreds.

4 Remove brisket from oven and let sit for 15 to 20 minutes. Pull brisket into shreds to use in tacos.

5 To make the tomatillo and cilantro salsa, in a mixing bowl, combine tomatillos, onions, cilantro, lime juice and salt. Gently fold in avocado. Cover and refrigerate until ready to serve.

6 To assemble tacos, place corn tortillas between damp paper towels and heat for 30 seconds in a microwave. Arrange hot tortillas on a platter and fill each with a generous portion of the brisket. Serve with tomatillo and cilantro salsa.

NUTRITION PER SERVING
(3 tacos)

Calories: 722

Fat: 13g

Sat Fat: 15g

Cholesterol: 151mg

Sodium: 2,144mg

Carbs: 92g

Fiber: 6g

Sugars: 52g

Protein: 57g

Spiced Bourbon Carnitas Tacos

YIELD
6 servings
(3 tacos per
serving)

PREP TIME
15 minutes

TOTAL TIME
2 hours
30 minutes

These braised pork tacos are a lively reincarnation of a bourbon smash, a cocktail featuring both orange juice and bourbon. Turn up the sweet heat with the harvest peach pico de gallo, a freshly chopped salsa featuring peaches, tomatoes, red onion, lime juice and jalapeño. This Mexican-inspired entrée is equal parts sweet, spice and fun. (See photo on pages 148–149.)

FOR THE SPICED BOURBON CARNITAS TACOS

2 teaspoons ground cumin

2 teaspoons garlic powder

2 teaspoons coarse salt

1 teaspoon paprika

1 teaspoon pepper

3 pound boneless pork roast, cut into 3-inch cubes

2 tablespoons olive oil

1 cup bourbon

1 cup orange juice

1 tablespoon brown sugar

18 warmed corn tortillas

FOR THE HARVEST PEACH PICO DE GALLO

2 cups finely diced peaches

1 cup finely diced roma tomatoes

½ cup finely diced red onion

¼ cup finely minced cilantro

2 tablespoons lime juice

1 teaspoon finely minced jalapeño

¼ teaspoon salt

1 Preheat oven to 350°F.

2 To make the spiced bourbon carnitas tacos, in a small mixing bowl, combine cumin, garlic powder, salt, paprika and pepper. Mix well and then evenly coat each piece of pork on all sides with the dry rub.

3 In a Dutch oven or heavy bottomed pot, heat olive oil over medium-high heat. Add seasoned pork pieces and sear on all sides until browned, about 2 minutes per side. Remove pork pieces from the Dutch oven or pot and set aside.

4 Add bourbon to deglaze the pan. Scrape up browned bits and then add orange juice and brown sugar.

5 Bring orange juice and bourbon mixture to a boil and then add back in the pork pieces. Cover Dutch oven or pot and place in the oven for 1 hour and 20 minutes. Turn pork pieces over and cook an additional 40 minutes uncovered or until pork is fork tender.

6 To make the harvest peach pico de gallo, in a mixing bowl, combine all ingredients and gently toss together. Cover and refrigerate until ready to serve.

7 Remove pork from oven and shred into thin pieces. Toss with remaining bourbon sauce left in the pot and then evenly distribute pork among heated corn tortillas. Serve with harvest peach pico de gallo.

NUTRITION PER SERVING
(3 tacos)

Calories: 690

Fat: 17g

Sat Fat: 4g

Cholesterol: 130mg

Sodium: 1,060mg

Carbs: 60g

Fiber: 5g

Sugars: 12g

Protein: 53g

YIELD
1 sandwich

PREP TIME
15 minutes

TOTAL TIME
20 minutes

Apricot Pesto Turkey Melt Sandwich

Though pesto is usually made with basil, pine nuts, Parmesan cheese and olive oil, this version breaks from tradition. Apricots take it to a sweeter dimension. If you have leftover pesto, toss it with some freshly cooked gluten-free pasta or eat it with cheese and crackers. For the sandwich, use the White Sandwich Bread on page 59 or the Multigrain Sandwich Bread on page 60.

FOR THE APRICOT PESTO

2 cups fresh basil, loosely packed

¼ cup chopped macadamia nuts

½ cup chopped dried apricots

½ cup olive oil

Salt, to taste

Pepper, to taste

FOR THE SANDWICH

2 teaspoons butter

2 slices gluten-free sandwich bread

1 tablespoon apricot pesto

4 ounces sliced turkey

1 slice smoked Gouda cheese

1 To make the apricot pesto, place basil in a food processor and pulse until leaves are roughly chopped. Add macadamia nuts and apricots to the processor and process until a rough paste forms.

2 With processor running, stream in olive oil until pesto is thick and oil is incorporated. Season to taste with salt and pepper.

3 To make the sandwich, heat a nonstick skillet or griddle over medium-high heat. Butter 1 side of each slice of bread.

4 Spread 1 tablespoon apricot pesto onto unbuttered side of bread slices. On 1 slice, place turkey and Gouda cheese and gently top with other bread slice.

5 Place on hot skillet or griddle and press down with a spatula. Cook for 2 to 3 minutes per side until golden and cheese is melted. Serve immediately.

NUTRITION PER SERVING

Calories: 600

Fat: 40g

Sat Fat: 11g

Cholesterol: 85mg

Sodium: 1,710mg

Carbs: 33g

Fiber: 2g

Sugars: 9g

Protein: 30g

⭐ Creamy Chicken & Spinach Enchilada Casserole

YIELD
6 servings

PREP TIME
15 minutes

TOTAL TIME
45 minutes

Impress the potluck with this Mexican-inspired and protein-rich layered casserole dish. Black beans and spinach are known for their high protein content and are notoriously filling, especially when loaded with corn tortillas and a tasty, creamy cheese sauce.

3 tablespoons olive oil, divided

1 large sweet yellow onion, diced

1 (8 ounce) package button mushrooms, thinly sliced

4 cloves garlic, minced

4 cups cooked shredded rotisserie chicken

4 cups lightly packed fresh spinach leaves

½ cup chicken stock

1 (8 ounce) package cream cheese

½ cup chopped cilantro

2 cups grated cheddar Jack cheese blend, divided

1 teaspoon salt

½ teaspoon chili powder

Nonstick cooking spray, for greasing casserole dish

18 corn tortillas

1 (15.5 ounce) can black beans, drained

1 Preheat oven to 375°F. In a large nonstick skillet, heat 2 tablespoons olive oil over medium-high heat. Add onions and mushrooms and sauté, stirring occasionally, until mushrooms begin to brown and onions are soft, about 5 to 7 minutes. Add garlic and cook 1 additional minute.

2 Add remaining 1 tablespoon of olive oil, chicken and spinach and cook, stirring frequently, until spinach has wilted.

3 Add chicken stock and bring to a boil. Add cream cheese and swirl cheese until it melts completely and a creamy sauce begins to form. Stir in cilantro, ½ cup cheese blend, salt and chili powder. Lower heat to medium-low and simmer for 3 minutes.

4 Spray a 9 x 13-inch casserole dish with nonstick cooking spray. Layer 6 corn tortillas along the bottom of the dish. Pour chicken and spinach mixture on top of the tortillas and spread out in an even layer. Top this layer with 6 more corn tortillas.

5 Pour black beans over tortillas to make the next layer. Sprinkle ½ cup cheese blend on top of the beans and then top with 6 more corn tortillas. Sprinkle remaining 1 cup of cheese blend on top of the casserole.

6 Bake for 20 to 22 minutes until cheese is bubbly and golden brown. Serve with guacamole and salsa, if desired.

NUTRITION PER SERVING

Calories: 1,240

Fat: 91g

Sat Fat: 31g

Cholesterol: 290mg

Sodium: 1,700mg

Carbs: 62g

Fiber: 7g

Sugars: 3g

Protein: 46g

⊛ Chicken & Biscuits

YIELD
8 to 10 servings

PREP TIME
1 hour

TOTAL TIME
1 hour
30 minutes

This gluten-free version of chicken and biscuits is every bit as down-home as the original. The chicken is sautéed with butternut squash, cremini mushrooms and green peas and seasoned with garlic, thyme and rosemary, then baked in a casserole-style dish with homemade gluten-free biscuit dough on top.

NUTRITION PER SERVING

Calories: 690

Fat: 32g

Sat Fat: 14g

Cholesterol: 175mg

Sodium: 1,160mg

Carbs: 54g

Fiber: 9g

Sugars: 11g

Protein: 48g

FOR THE BISCUITS

2 ½ cups gluten-free all-purpose flour, plus additional for rolling out

1 ½ teaspoons baking powder

1 teaspoon salt

½ teaspoon fresh rosemary

1 egg, beaten

¾ cup milk

½ teaspoon apple cider vinegar

¾ cup cold butter (1 ½ sticks), cut into cubes

FOR THE CHICKEN

4 tablespoons olive oil

1 medium yellow onion, diced

4 carrots, cut into rounds

4 cloves garlic, minced

2 teaspoons dried thyme

1 teaspoon minced fresh rosemary

2 cups diced butternut squash

2 cups sliced cremini mushrooms

2 cups green peas (fresh or frozen)

2 pounds chicken breast, cooked and shredded or diced

4 cups chicken stock

⅓ cup gluten-free all-purpose flour

Salt, to taste

Pepper, to taste

1 To make the biscuits, in a large bowl combine gluten-free all-purpose flour, baking powder, salt and rosemary and whisk to incorporate. In a separate bowl, mix together egg, milk and apple cider vinegar.

2 Using fingers, cut butter into flour mixture until it is the size of small pebbles.

3 Make a small well in the flour mixture and add egg mixture. Gently combine with a fork until just moistened.

4 Knead together with hands and roll out on floured surface until dough is about 1 ½ inches thick. Cut out biscuits with a biscuit cutter and set them on a baking sheet. Keep refrigerated until ready to bake.

5 To make the chicken, preheat oven to 375°F. In a large, deep pot, heat olive oil over medium-high heat. Add onions and carrots and sauté for about 7 minutes until softened.

6 Add garlic, thyme and rosemary and sauté another 2 to 3 minutes. Add squash, mushrooms and peas and stir to combine. Sauté for 10 minutes until softened.

7 Add chicken and gently stir to combine. Add chicken stock and bring to a boil, then reduce to a simmer. Simmer for 15 minutes.

8 Add gluten-free all-purpose flour to the hot liquid and whisk vigorously to thicken. Continue to whisk until flour is fully dissolved. Season with salt and pepper to taste.

9 Pour chicken filling into a 9 x 13-inch baking dish. Add biscuits from refrigerator on top.

10 Bake for 35 to 45 minutes until biscuits are golden and chicken filling is bubbling. Cool slightly before serving.

YIELD
4 servings
(2 skewers
per serving)

PREP TIME
10 minutes

TOTAL TIME
20 minutes

Chicken Satay with Peanut Sauce

Grill in Thai style with this simple chicken satay seasoned with lime juice and a side of creamy peanut sauce with a touch of heat from crushed red pepper flakes. Be sure to soak your skewers before throwing the chicken on the grill so they don't catch fire. Serve them at your next backyard party for an instant party pleaser!

FOR THE PEANUT SAUCE

¼ cup creamy peanut butter

¼ cup coconut milk

2 tablespoons lime juice

1 tablespoon gluten-free soy sauce

2 teaspoons brown sugar

½ teaspoon crushed red pepper flakes

FOR THE CHICKEN SATAY

12 chicken tender pieces

8 wooden skewers, soaked in water for at least 10 minutes

¼ cup lime juice

1 teaspoon salt, plus additional if needed

1 teaspoon garlic powder, plus additional if needed

1 teaspoon pepper, plus additional if needed

1 To make the peanut sauce, in a mixing bowl, whisk together peanut butter, coconut milk, lime juice, gluten-free soy sauce, brown sugar and red pepper flakes until a smooth sauce forms. Cover and chill until ready to serve.

2 To make the chicken satay, preheat grill over high heat. Thread each chicken tender piece through a soaked wooden skewer. Drizzle lime juice over each piece of chicken and then sprinkle each piece with salt, garlic powder and pepper.

3 Cook each chicken skewer on the heated grill for approximately 3 minutes per side until chicken reaches an internal temperature of 165°F and the juices run clear.

4 Serve chicken satay with peanut sauce.

NUTRITION PER SERVING
(2 skewers)

Calories: 490

Fat: 24g

Sat Fat: 6g

Cholesterol: 50mg

Sodium: 1,840mg

Carbs: 34g

Fiber: 4g

Sugars: 7g

Protein: 35g

Coconut Curry & Pineapple Shrimp

Shrimp, snow peas and pineapple dance in this coconut milk–based curry made with red curry paste. The red curry paste has a little heat from red chili and tanginess from lemongrass. Serve it on a bed of rice for an Asian-inspired dish that's both light and flavorful. Don't have fresh pineapple on hand? Frozen or canned is fine, but be sure to drain the juice before throwing it into the curry.

3 tablespoons olive oil, divided

1 pound shrimp, peeled and deveined

1 medium yellow onion, chopped

1 teaspoon minced garlic

1 ½ tablespoons red curry paste

1 (14 ounce) can coconut milk

¼ cup chicken stock

2 tablespoons fish sauce

2 tablespoons brown sugar

1 tablespoon lime juice

2 cups snow peas

1 cup chopped pineapple

Steamed white or brown rice, for serving

1 In a large nonstick skillet, heat 1 tablespoon olive oil over medium-high heat. Add shrimp and cook, stirring occasionally, for 4 to 5 minutes until shrimp are pink and lightly browned. Remove shrimp from skillet and set aside.

2 To the same skillet, add remaining 2 tablespoons of olive oil and heat over medium-high heat. Add onions and cook, stirring occasionally, until onions are translucent, about 5 to 7 minutes. Add garlic and cook 1 additional minute until fragrant.

3 Add red curry paste and coconut milk and stir mixture until curry paste is completely dissolved in the liquid. Bring mixture to a slow simmer and then stir in chicken stock, fish sauce, brown sugar and lime juice. Simmer, stirring frequently, for 3 to 4 minutes.

4 Reduce heat to medium low and add snow peas, pineapple and cooked shrimp. Cook for 3 to 5 minutes, just until shrimp are heated and peas are soft.

5 Serve curry on top of steamed white or brown rice.

Calories: 590

Fat: 29g

Sat Fat: 18g

Cholesterol: 14.5mg

Sodium: 1,480mg

Carbs: 61g

Fiber: 3g

Sugars: 18g

Protein: 23g

Flaky Cheddar Beef Potpies

YIELD
6 servings

PREP TIME
45 minutes

TOTAL TIME
1 hour
15 minutes

Flaky biscuits top this hearty beef stew. It's the most wonderful dish to eat on a cold winter night.

FOR THE FLAKY CHEDDAR CRUST

2 ½ cups gluten-free all-purpose flour

1 teaspoon salt

½ teaspoon garlic powder

1 ½ cups grated sharp cheddar cheese

¾ cup (1 ½ sticks) cold butter, cut into small pieces

½ cup ice water

Plastic wrap, to cover dough

FOR THE STEW

4 tablespoons butter, divided

1 ½ pounds beef (sirloin tip or chuck roast), cut into bite-sized cubes

1 cup finely chopped sweet yellow onion

1 pound thinly sliced button mushrooms,

2 cups thinly sliced leeks, white and light green parts only

1 cup finely chopped carrots

2 cups beef stock

½ cup milk

½ cup red wine

3 tablespoons cornstarch

2 teaspoons sea salt

1 cup frozen green peas

1 egg, beaten lightly with 1 tablespoon water for egg wash

1 To make the flaky cheddar crust, in a food processor add gluten-free all-purpose flour, salt and garlic powder. Pulse until light and well mixed. Add cheddar cheese and butter and process until the mixture resembles pea-sized crumbles. Slowly pulse in ice water until the dough pulls together.

2 Roll dough into a ball and wrap in plastic wrap. Press down into a disk and refrigerate for 30 minutes.

3 To make the stew, in a large pot, melt 2 tablespoons butter over medium-high heat. Add beef and cook, stirring occasionally, until beef is browned on all sides. Remove beef from pot and set aside.

4 To the same pot, add remaining 2 tablespoons of butter and heat over medium-high heat. Add onions, mushrooms, leeks and carrots and cook, stirring occasionally, for 7 to 9 minutes until onions and mushrooms are lightly browned.

5 In a measuring cup, whisk together beef stock, milk, red wine, cornstarch and sea salt. Pour liquid over the vegetables and stir to combine well. Bring to a boil and cook, stirring constantly, until mixture thickens, about 3 to 4 minutes.

6 Stir in browned beef and green peas and mix well. Remove from heat and cool for 15 minutes.

7 Preheat oven to 350°F. Set 6 (8 ounce) ramekins on a baking sheet and divide cooled beef mixture evenly among them. Cut out 6 circles from the crust dough that are just slightly larger than the top of each ramekin.

8 Prepare egg wash and lightly brush the top rim of each ramekin. Press one pie crust circle on top of each ramekin and press down lightly to seal the edges.

9 Cut small slits in the top of each circle for venting and then brush the entire surface with egg wash. Bake for 25 minutes until lightly golden. Serve immediately.

NUTRITION PER SERVING

Calories: 890

Fat: 59g

Sat Fat: 32g

Cholesterol: 200mg

Sodium: 1,880mg

Carbs: 60g

Fiber: 9g

Sugars: 9g

Protein: 34g

Ground Turkey Stuffed Bell Peppers

These veggie and turkey stuffed bell peppers are so tasty and good for you, too! Zucchini, carrots and corn mixed with feta cheese and browned ground turkey fill out the hollowed peppers and are baked with a layer of marinara sauce. Serve with a side of rice or quinoa to round out the meal.

YIELD
4 servings
(2 bell
peppers per
serving)

PREP TIME
20 minutes

TOTAL TIME
1 hour
5 minutes

Foil, for lining baking dish

2 tablespoons olive oil

1 pound thinly sliced button mushrooms

1 sweet yellow onion, finely diced

1 pound ground turkey

1 egg, lightly beaten

1 zucchini, ends removed and shredded

1 carrot, shredded

1 (8.75 ounce) can sweet corn kernels

1 cup crumbled feta cheese

1 teaspoon salt

1 teaspoon garlic powder

1 (24 ounce) jar marinara sauce

8 bell peppers (red, yellow, orange or green)

2 cups grated Parmesan cheese

1 Preheat the oven to 375°F. Line a 9 x 13-inch glass baking dish with foil and set aside.

2 In a sauté pan, heat olive oil over medium-high heat. Add mushrooms and onions and sauté until lightly browned, about 5 to 7 minutes. Remove from heat and set aside.

3 In a bowl, mix together ground turkey, egg, zucchini, carrots, corn, feta cheese, salt and garlic powder. Stir sautéed mushrooms and onions into this mixture.

4 Pour approximately ½ cup marinara sauce into the bottom of prepared baking dish and spread out to form an even layer.

5 Slice tops off bell peppers, clean out core and seeds and place them in prepared baking dish, top facing up. Stuff turkey mixture evenly into each of the peppers.

6 Drizzle remaining marinara sauce evenly on top of each stuffed pepper.

7 Bake for 30 minutes. Remove from oven and sprinkle Parmesan cheese on top of peppers. Cook an additional 10 to 15 minutes until cheese melts and is golden brown.

8 Serve ground turkey stuffed bell peppers with a side dish of rice or quinoa.

NUTRITION PER SERVING
(2 bell peppers)

Calories: 920

Fat: 52g

Sat Fat: 20g

Cholesterol: 215mg

Sodium: 2,940mg

Carbs: 61g

Fiber: 10g

Sugars: 17g

Protein: 61g

Desserts

Banana Split Cupcakes – page 210

YIELD
12 servings

PREP TIME
15 minutes

TOTAL TIME
3 hours
15 minutes

Chocolate Chip Peanut Butter Cookie Cheesecake

Can't decide between cookies and cheesecake? Now you don't have to! This traditional cheesecake filling sits on top of a chocolate chip cookie crust. The recipe below is for simple chocolate chip cookie dough, but you could make this recipe an infinite number of ways by simply picking another type of cookie. Perhaps try gingersnaps, lemon sugar cookies or even a crust made from white chocolate cranberry cookie dough. The possibilities are endless! Store leftover cheesecake in an airtight container in the refrigerator for up to three days.

FOR THE CRUST

Nonstick cooking spray, for greasing springform pan

2 ¼ cups gluten-free all-purpose flour

1 teaspoon baking powder

1 teaspoon salt

1 cup (2 sticks) butter, room temperature

¾ cup sugar

¾ cup brown sugar

2 teaspoons vanilla extract

2 eggs

1 cup semisweet chocolate chips

Plastic wrap, for covering dough

FOR THE CHEESECAKE

3 (8 ounce) packages cream cheese

3 eggs

1 cup sugar

3 teaspoons vanilla extract

1 Preheat oven to 350°F. Grease the bottom of an 8-inch springform pan with nonstick cooking spray and set aside.

2 To make the crust, in a mixing bowl, whisk together gluten-free all-purpose flour, baking powder and salt.

3 In the bowl of a stand mixer using the paddle attachment, cream together butter, sugar and brown sugar until light and creamy. Add vanilla extract and eggs and mix well. Slowly add dry ingredients into the wet ingredients, mixing well after each addition. Add chocolate chips and mix gently.

4 Roll crust dough into a large ball and wrap in plastic wrap. Refrigerate for 20 minutes.

5 To make the cheesecake, in the bowl of a stand mixer using the paddle attachment, mix together cream cheese, eggs, sugar and vanilla extract. Beat until light and fluffy.

6 Remove dough from refrigerator and cut off approximately ½ cup of dough. Set aside. Press remaining dough snuggly into the bottom of prepared springform pan. Pour cream cheese batter over top of the crust.

7 Crumble reserved cookie dough into small pieces and spread evenly across the top of the cheesecake.

8 Bake for 50 to 55 minutes until center of the cheesecake is fully set. Cool on counter to room temperature and then chill in the refrigerator for 2 hours before cutting.

NUTRITION PER SERVING

Calories: 800

Fat: 50g

Sat Fat: 29g

Cholesterol: 230mg

Sodium: 700mg

Carbs: 84g

Fiber: 4g

Sugars: 62g

Protein: 11g

YIELD
5 servings
(10 crepes)

PREP TIME
35 minutes

TOTAL TIME
45 minutes

Buckwheat Crepes with Mascarpone Orange Crème & Fresh Peaches

Sweet and creamy orange-infused Mascarpone lines these buckwheat crepes filled with peaches. This dessert is fresh and light enough to satisfy your summertime sweet tooth!

FOR THE CREPE BATTER

5 tablespoons butter, melted

1 cup buckwheat flour

2 tablespoons cornstarch

1 tablespoon sugar

2 cups milk

3 eggs

½ teaspoon salt

FOR THE FILLING

Nonstick cooking spray, for greasing skillet

1 (8 ounce) container Mascarpone cheese

2 tablespoons ricotta cheese

¼ cup honey

2 teaspoons orange zest

2 teaspoons orange juice

2 large peaches, pitted and thinly sliced

Powdered sugar, for garnish

1 To make the crepe batter, in a blender or food processor, combine melted butter, buckwheat flour, cornstarch, sugar, milk, eggs and salt. Purée until a smooth batter forms. Cover and refrigerate for 30 minutes.

2 Heat a 10.75-inch nonstick skillet over medium heat and spray with nonstick cooking spray. Pour ⅓ cup of batter into skillet and cook for about 2 minutes until the crepe sets and the edges begin to brown. Carefully flip crepe over and cook an additional 2 minutes. Set finished crepe aside and repeat process until all the batter is cooked into crepes.

3 To make the filling, in the bowl of a stand mixer using the paddle attachment, beat together Mascarpone, ricotta, honey, orange zest and orange juice until a creamy mixture forms.

4 Evenly divide Mascarpone mixture among the crepes and spread into a thin layer. Divide peaches between each of the crepes and then roll up.

5 Garnish crepes with powdered sugar before serving.

NUTRITION PER SERVING
(2 crepes)

Calories: 590

Fat: 38g

Sat Fat: 21g

Cholesterol: 225mg

Sodium: 450mg

Carbs: 51g

Fiber: 5g

Sugars: 28g

Protein: 15g

FAN FAVORITE

YIELD
24 truffles

PREP TIME
5 minutes

TOTAL TIME
15 minutes

Peanut Butter & Agave Nectar Truffles

Just three simple ingredients make up these mouthwatering truffles. If dairy is an issue in your family, substitute soy powder for the milk powder. Live in a peanut-free zone? No problem! Substitute almond butter or Nutella for the peanut butter. Store leftover truffles in an airtight container in the refrigerator for up to one week.

¾ cup dry milk powder

1 cup creamy peanut butter

¼ cup agave nectar

Topping suggestions: coconut flakes, crushed nuts, cinnamon sugar, cocoa powder, sprinkles or chopped dried fruit

1 In the bowl of a stand mixer using the paddle attachment, beat together dry milk powder, peanut butter and agave nectar until they form into a very soft, smooth dough.

2 Set up selected toppings in individual shallow bowls.

3 Roll dough into 1-inch balls and then roll into desired toppings.

4 Refrigerate truffles for 30 minutes to harden before serving.

NUTRITION PER SERVING
(1 truffle)

Calories: 370

Fat: 25g

Sat Fat: 9g

Cholesterol: 10mg

Sodium: 200mg

Carbs: 26g

Fiber: 3g

Sugars: 20g

Protein: 11g

YIELD
12 servings

PREP TIME
15 minutes

TOTAL TIME
50 minutes

Lemon Lime Bars

Not your average lemon bars! Bursting with flavors of both lemons and limes, these cookie bars are great for a summertime dessert. Store leftovers in an airtight container for up to one week.

FOR THE CRUST

2 cups gluten-free all-purpose flour

½ cup powdered sugar, plus additional for topping

1 cup (2 sticks) butter, each cut into 5 pieces

FOR THE FILLING

2 cups sugar

4 eggs, beaten

⅔ cup lemon juice

⅓ cup lime juice

1 tablespoon lemon zest

½ tablespoon lime zest

2 ½ tablespoons cornstarch

1 ½ teaspoons baking powder

½ teaspoon salt

Powdered sugar, for garnish

1 Preheat oven to 300°F.

2 To make the crust, in the bowl of a food processor, pulse together gluten-free all-purpose flour and powdered sugar. Add butter until well blended. Press crust into the bottom of a 9 x 13-inch glass baking dish. Bake crust for 25 minutes until lightly golden. Remove from oven and cool.

3 To make the filling, in a mixing bowl, whisk together sugar, eggs, lemon juice, lime juice, lemon zest, lime zest, cornstarch, baking powder and salt. Continue whisking until a smooth mixture forms. Pour filling on top of the cooled crust.

4 Increase oven temperature to 350°F. Bake lemon lime bars for 28 to 30 minutes until the filling sets. Dust with powdered sugar before serving.

NUTRITION PER SERVING

Calories: 390

Fat: 17g

Sat Fat: 10g

Cholesterol: 110mg

Sodium: 320mg

Carbs: 57g

Fiber: 2g

Sugars: 40g

Protein: 4g

YIELD
12 servings

PREP TIME
5 minutes

TOTAL TIME
2 hours
5 minutes

NUTRITION PER SERVING

Calories: 420

Fat: 26g

Sat Fat: 18g

Cholesterol: 5mg

Sodium: 720mg

Carbs: 47g

Fiber: 3g

Sugars: 43g

Protein: 6g

White & Dark Chocolate Bark with Crushed Pistachios & Sea Salt

Sweet and salty flavors come together in this chocolate bark recipe. This recipe works great as a homemade holiday gift. Make several batches, wrap the bark in festive containers and share it with your friends and family for the holidays.

Foil and nonstick cooking spray, for lining and greasing baking dish

1 pound dark chocolate, chopped into small pieces

2 tablespoons butter, divided

1 pound white chocolate, chopped into small pieces

½ cup crushed pistachios

1 tablespoon sea salt

1 Line a 9 x 13-inch baking dish with foil and lightly spray with nonstick cooking spray and set aside.

2 In a double boiler, melt dark chocolate pieces and 1 tablespoon butter. Pour chocolate onto prepared baking dish and spread into an even layer. Set aside for 15 minutes until firmly set.

3 In a double boiler, melt white chocolate pieces and remaining 1 tablespoon of butter. Pour white chocolate on top of the dark chocolate and spread into an even layer. Immediately sprinkle pistachios and sea salt on top of the white chocolate layer.

4 Let bark set at room temperature for 1 hour to 1 hour and 30 minutes. Once set, lift bark out of the baking dish and break it into bite-sized pieces. Store for up to 1 week in an airtight container.

YIELD
24 cookies

PREP TIME
15 minutes

TOTAL TIME
35 minutes

White Chocolate Coconut Oat Cookies

Gluten-free oats and coconut flour form the starchy base of these cookies. Be sure to select oats that are certified as gluten-free. Many brands of oats are produced in facilities where cross-contamination can occur, so make sure to pick up a trusted brand.

Parchment paper and nonstick cooking spray, for lining and greasing baking sheet

1 cup (2 sticks) butter

1 ⅓ cups sugar

2 teaspoons vanilla extract

2 cups quick cook gluten-free oats

½ cup coconut flour

1 teaspoon salt

2 egg whites, lightly beaten

1 cup white chocolate chips, melted

1 Preheat oven to 350°F. Line a baking sheet with parchment paper and lightly spray with nonstick cooking spray and set aside.

2 In a small pot over medium heat, melt together butter and sugar. Once sugar has fully dissolved, about 7 minutes, whisk in vanilla extract.

3 Pour mixture into a large mixing bowl and mix in gluten-free oats, coconut flour and salt. Let dough sit for 5 minutes and then fold in egg whites.

4 Drop dough by tablespoonful onto prepared baking sheet and flatten each cookie with a fork. Bake for 14 to 16 minutes until golden. Cool on baking sheet until cookies are firm.

5 Once cookies have cooled, drizzle melted white chocolate on top. Let set before serving.

NUTRITION PER SERVING
(1 cookie)

Calories: 210

Fat: 11g

Sat Fat: 8g

Cholesterol: 20mg

Sodium: 200mg

Carbs: 23g

Fiber: 2g

Sugars: 18g

Protein: 3g

Cranberry White Chocolate Chunk Biscotti

Whole blanched almonds and cornmeal make these naturally gluten-free biscotti delightfully crunchy. Wrap any leftover biscotti tightly with foil and store on the counter for up to one week.

Nonstick cooking spray, for greasing baking pan

2 cups whole blanched almonds

1 cup yellow cornmeal

1 cup cornstarch

½ teaspoon baking soda

½ teaspoon ground cinnamon

1 egg

⅔ cup sugar

¼ cup honey

2 tablespoons melted butter

1 teaspoon vanilla extract

½ cup chopped dried cranberries

½ cup chopped white chocolate pieces

1 Preheat oven to 350°F and set rack in middle of the oven. Grease a 9 x 13-inch baking pan with nonstick cooking spray and set aside.

2 In a food processor, pulse almonds until they are finely ground. Place ground almonds into a mixing bowl and mix in cornmeal, cornstarch, baking soda and cinnamon. Mix until well combined.

3 In the bowl of a stand mixer using the paddle attachment, beat together egg, sugar, honey, melted butter and vanilla extract. Slowly add dry ingredients into the wet ingredients and mix until a stiff dough forms. Add dried cranberries and white chocolate pieces.

4 Press dough into an even layer on prepared baking pan using the palm of your hand. The dough should be approximately ½ inch thick.

5 Bake for 30 minutes until firm. Remove from oven and cool for 5 minutes. Carefully invert biscotti block onto a cutting board and cool completely.

6 Cut biscotti into 3 long strips and then slice each strip into individual cookies, about ½ inch thick. Place cut cookies back on baking pan and bake an additional 15 minutes until crispy.

NUTRITION PER SERVING
(1 cookie)

Calories: 180

Fat: 9g

Sat Fat: 2.5g

Cholesterol: 10mg

Sodium: 55mg

Carbs: 23g

Fiber: 2g

Sugars: 12g

Protein: 4g

Vanilla Pound Cake with Lemon Basil Sorbet & Fresh Strawberries

Light and fresh lemon basil sorbet beautifully accents this sweet pound cake. If you don't have an ice cream maker, freeze the sorbet in a freezer-safe container and stir every two hours to keep a smooth texture.

FOR THE LEMON BASIL SORBET

2 cups water

1 ½ cups sugar

2 tablespoons lemon zest

1 ½ cups fresh basil leaves, very finely chopped

¼ teaspoon salt

2 cups lemon juice

FOR THE VANILLA POUND CAKE BATTER

Nonstick cooking spray, for greasing loaf pan

1 cup (2 sticks) butter, softened

½ cup granulated sugar

½ cup powdered sugar

4 eggs

2 teaspoons vanilla extract

1 teaspoon lemon zest

1 teaspoon salt

2 cups gluten-free all-purpose flour

4 cups freshly sliced strawberries

1 To make the lemon basil sorbet, in a small pot, whisk together water, sugar and lemon zest. Cook over medium-low heat until sugar is fully dissolved and the mixture comes to a slow simmer. Remove from heat and whisk in basil and salt. Cool completely and then stir in lemon juice.

2 Refrigerate mixture for 2 hours before transferring to an ice cream maker and processing per machine instructions. Cover and freeze until ready to serve with the pound cake.

3 To make the vanilla pound cake batter, preheat oven to 350°F. Grease a loaf pan with nonstick cooking spray and set aside.

4 In the bowl of a stand mixer using the paddle attachment, cream together butter and sugars. Add eggs one at a time, beating well after each addition. Add vanilla extract, lemon zest and salt and mix well.

5 Slowly add gluten-free all-purpose flour and mix until well combined.

6 Pour batter into prepared loaf pan and bake for 55 to 65 minutes until a toothpick inserted into the center of the pound cake comes out clean. Cool on a wire rack until completely cooled.

7 Slice the vanilla pound cake into 8 slices and arrange 1 slice on each serving plate. Top with a heaping scoop of lemon basil sorbet and a large spoonful of fresh strawberries.

YIELD
8 servings

PREP TIME
15 minutes

TOTAL TIME
3 hours (includes chilling time)

NUTRITION PER SERVING

Calories: 570

Fat: 24g

Sat Fat: 15g

Cholesterol: 60mg

Sodium: 570mg

Carbs: 90g

Fiber: 5g

Sugars: 64g

Protein: 4g

YIELD
10 servings

PREP TIME
15 minutes

TOTAL TIME
50 minutes

Apple Carrot Cake with Vanilla Cream Cheese Frosting

This cake is packed with fresh carrots and apples and works great for breakfast with a cup of coffee or as an after-dinner dessert.

FOR THE APPLE CARROT CAKE BATTER

Nonstick cooking spray, for greasing bundt pan

2 cups almond flour

½ cup tapioca flour or potato starch

1 ½ teaspoons ground cinnamon

1 teaspoon ground ginger

1 teaspoon baking powder

½ teaspoon sea salt

3 egg whites

2 whole eggs

1 ½ cups sugar

1 ½ cups shredded carrots

1 cup shredded green apple

1 tablespoon orange zest

FOR THE VANILLA CREAM CHEESE FROSTING

1 (8 ounce) package cream cheese, room temperature

½ cup (1 stick) butter, room temperature

2 cups powdered sugar

2 teaspoons vanilla extract

¼ teaspoon salt

1 Preheat oven to 375°F. Grease a bundt pan with nonstick cooking spray and set aside.

2 To make the apple carrot cake batter, in a mixing bowl, whisk together almond flour, tapioca flour or potato starch, cinnamon, ginger, baking powder and sea salt. Mix together well and set aside.

3 In the bowl of a stand mixer using the whisk attachment, beat egg whites until stiff peaks form. Carefully transfer into a separate bowl and set aside.

4 In the stand mixer using the paddle attachment, mix together whole eggs and sugar until light and fluffy, about 3 to 4 minutes. Add carrots, green apple and orange zest and mix until well combined.

5 Slowly add dry ingredients into the wet ingredients and mix until well combined. Using a spatula, gently fold prepared egg whites into the batter.

6 Pour batter into prepared bundt pan and bake for 28 to 32 minutes until a toothpick inserted into the center of the cake comes out clean.

7 To make the vanilla cream cheese frosting, whisk together all ingredients until smooth. Drizzle as desired over the apple carrot cake before serving.

NUTRITION PER SERVING

Calories: 550

Fat: 28g

Sat Fat: 11g

Cholesterol: 50mg

Sodium: 420mg

Carbs: 72g

Fiber: 3g

Sugars: 57g

Protein: 8g

Blackberry Peach Galette

A simple filling made from blackberry preserves and sliced peaches accent this summertime galette. Store leftovers in the refrigerator in an airtight container for up to three days.

FOR THE CRUST

½ cup (1 stick) cold butter, cut into small pieces

1 ¼ cups gluten-free all-purpose flour plus additional for rolling out

½ teaspoon salt

¼ cup cold water

Plastic wrap, for covering dough

Parchment paper, for rolling out

FOR THE FILLING

¼ cup blackberry preserves

¼ teaspoon vanilla extract

1 pound peaches, thinly sliced

1 To make the crust, place butter in the freezer for 15 to 20 minutes before making dough. In a food processor, pulse gluten-free all-purpose flour and salt to aerate. Add cold butter and pulse until there are no butter pieces larger than a pea. Add water, 2 tablespoons at a time, pulsing in between additions. Add water until mixture resembles large curds.

2 Turn pie dough out onto plastic wrap. Gently use plastic wrap and hands to form dough into a disk. The mixture may be slightly crumbly. Chill in refrigerator for at least 2 hours before using. Bring to a cool room temperature before rolling out.

3 Roll out pie dough to a 12-inch circle on gluten-free floured parchment paper and put on a baking sheet and set aside.

4 To make the filling, in a small bowl, stir together blackberry preserves and vanilla extract. Using a pastry brush, gently brush preserves onto pie dough, leaving a 2-inch perimeter around the edges.

5 Place peach slices on dough in a circular pattern, working from the outside to the inside.

6 Gently fold over edges of the dough, using parchment paper to help if needed. Pinch together creases with your fingers, sealing the dough. Chill for at least 1 hour before baking.

7 Preheat oven to 425°F. Bake blackberry peach galette for 10 minutes. Lower heat to 375°F and continue to bake for another 35 to 40 minutes until preserves bubble and crust is golden brown. Cool completely before serving.

 FAN FAVORITE

YIELD
8 servings

PREP TIME
30 minutes

TOTAL TIME
2 hours
30 minutes

NUTRITION PER SERVING

Calories: 210

Fat: 12g

Sat Fat: 7g

Cholesterol: 30mg

Sodium: 135mg

Carbs: 26g

Fiber: 3g

Sugars: 11g

Protein: 3g

Caramel Apple & Blueberry Streusel Cake

 FAN FAVORITE

YIELD
12 servings

PREP TIME
30 minutes

TOTAL TIME
2 hours

This cake is sweet and tart at the same time. It combines the classic streusel coffee cake topping with the luscious flavors of a cobbler. Want to make your own caramel sauce instead of using a store-bought brand? Simply heat 1 cup brown sugar, ½ cup butter, ¼ cup heavy cream and ¼ cup agave nectar over medium-high heat until it comes to a boil, making sure to stir constantly. Let the mixture boil for 3 to 4 minutes, then remove it from the heat and cool until ready to use.

FOR THE APPLE AND BLUEBERRY TOPPING

Nonstick cooking spray or butter, for greasing springform pan

2 tablespoons butter

2 Granny Smith apples, cored and thinly sliced

1 cup blueberries

1 tablespoon sugar

FOR THE STREUSEL TOPPING

1 cup gluten-free all-purpose flour

1 cup walnuts or pecans

1 cup packed brown sugar

½ cup (1 stick) butter, melted

2 teaspoons ground cinnamon

½ teaspoon salt

FOR THE CAKE BATTER

½ cup (1 stick) butter, softened

1 cup granulated sugar

2 eggs

2 teaspoons vanilla extract

2 cups gluten-free all-purpose flour

2 teaspoons baking powder

1 teaspoon salt

⅔ cup milk, divided

½ cup caramel sauce

1 Preheat oven to 350°F. Grease a 9-inch springform pan with nonstick cooking spray or butter and set aside.

2 To make the apple and blueberry topping, heat butter in a nonstick skillet over medium-high heat. Add apples, blueberries and sugar and sauté for 5 to 7 minutes until fruit is soft. Remove from heat and cool.

3 To make the streusel topping, in the bowl of a food processor, combine gluten-free all-purpose flour, walnuts or pecans, brown sugar, melted butter, cinnamon and salt and pulse until a crumbly topping forms.

4 To make the cake batter, in the bowl of a stand mixer using the paddle attachment, cream together butter and sugar. Add eggs 1 at a time, mixing well after each addition. Add vanilla extract and mix well.

5 In a separate bowl, whisk together gluten-free all-purpose flour, baking powder and salt. Slowly add approximately ⅓ of dry ingredients into the wet ingredients and then add ⅓ cup milk. Add another ⅓ of dry ingredients and remaining ⅓ cup of milk. Mix well and add all remaining dry ingredients to the batter.

6 Pour batter into prepared springform pan. Top cake with cooled fruit and then sprinkle streusel crumble on top of the fruit. Drizzle caramel sauce on top of the cake.

7 Bake for 50 to 60 minutes until a toothpick inserted into the center of the cake comes out clean. Cool for 30 minutes before removing sides of the springform pan.

NUTRITION PER SERVING

Calories: 540

Fat: 27g

Sat Fat: 12g

Cholesterol: 85mg

Sodium: 570mg

Carbs: 75g

Fiber: 5g

Sugars: 46g

Protein: 7g

YIELD
6 servings

PREP TIME
5 minutes

TOTAL TIME
3 hours

Chocolate Peanut Butter Pudding Cups

This dairy-free pudding dessert is bursting with flavors of chocolate and peanut butter. If soy is an issue, replace the vanilla soymilk with 1% milk and add 1 teaspoon of vanilla extract. If you make this substitution, the recipe will no longer be considered dairy-free.

NUTRITION PER SERVING

Calories: 330

Fat: 18g

Sat Fat: 5g

Cholesterol: 0mg

Sodium: 115mg

Carbs: 39g

Fiber: 4g

Sugars: 24g

Protein: 10g

¼ cup cocoa powder

¼ cup sugar

2 tablespoons cornstarch

2 cups vanilla soymilk

¼ cup creamy peanut butter

¼ teaspoon salt

Plastic wrap, for covering bowl

½ cup crushed peanuts, for garnish

½ cup dairy-free chocolate shavings, for garnish

1 In a medium-sized saucepan, whisk together cocoa powder, sugar and cornstarch. Whisk in vanilla soymilk and heat over medium heat until mixture comes to a slow boil and begins to thicken, about 7 to 9 minutes.

2 Remove from heat and stir in peanut butter and salt. Pour into a bowl, cover with plastic wrap and cool for 2 to 3 hours in the refrigerator.

3 Spoon chilled pudding into 6 individual serving bowls and garnish each with crushed peanuts and chocolate shavings.

Maple Gingersnap Cheesecake with Caramelized Pears

This grain-free and egg-free cheesecake is the ultimate in lavish desserts. And it works beautifully for those nights when both gluten and egg allergies need to be accommodated. Just make sure to allow for plenty of chilling time before serving.

FOR THE CRUST

Nonstick cooking spray, for greasing springform pan

2 cups chopped walnuts

½ cup coconut flour

½ cup sugar

2 teaspoons ground ginger

6 tablespoons butter, melted

FOR THE CARMELIZED PEARS

Foil, for lining baking sheet

2 Bartlett pears, skin on, cored and thinly sliced

2 tablespoons maple syrup

FOR THE CHEESECAKE FILLING

2 cups heavy cream

½ cup granulated sugar

2 (8 ounce) packages cream cheese, softened

2 tablespoons powdered sugar

2 tablespoons maple syrup

2 teaspoons fresh lemon juice

1 teaspoon vanilla extract

1 Preheat oven to 350°F. Spray a 9-inch springform pan with nonstick cooking spray and set aside.

2 To make crust, in a food processor, combine walnuts, coconut flour, sugar, ginger and melted butter and pulse until finely ground into crumbs. Press mixture into the bottom and along the sides of prepared springform pan. Bake for 10 minutes. Remove from oven, cool and set aside.

3 Increase oven temperature to 425°F.

4 To make the carmelized pears, line a baking sheet with foil and arrange pear slices on the tray. Brush maple syrup across pear slices. Bake for 15 to 20 minutes until pears are soft and golden brown. Remove from oven and cool completely.

5 To make the cheesecake filling, in the bowl of a stand mixer using the whisk attachment, beat heavy cream and granulated sugar until stiff peaks form. Transfer to a separate bowl and set aside.

6 In the bowl of a stand mixer using the paddle attachment, mix together cream cheese, powdered sugar, maple syrup, lemon juice and vanilla extract. Mix on medium speed until well combined, light and fluffy. Reduce speed to slow and add whipped cream mixture.

7 Pour whipped cream cheese mixture on top of the crust. Arrange caramelized pears on top of cheesecake and refrigerate for 2 to 3 hours until fully set. Unmold cheesecake from the springform pan sides before serving.

YIELD
10 servings

PREP TIME
30 minutes

TOTAL TIME
3 hours
30 minutes

NUTRITION PER SERVING

Calories: 690

Fat: 56g

Sat Fat: 26g

Cholesterol: 135mg

Sodium: 240mg

Carbs: 44g

Fiber: 5g

Sugars: 34g

Protein: 8g

YIELD
12 servings

PREP TIME
30 minutes

TOTAL TIME
1 hour
30 minutes

Tres Leches Cake

The gluten-free version of this traditional Latin cake is rich, delicious and makes the perfect cake for a summer party.

FOR THE CAKE BATTER

Nonstick cooking spray, for greasing cake pan

¾ cup brown rice flour

⅓ cup white rice flour

¼ cup potato starch

1 teaspoon baking powder

½ teaspoon xanthan gum

¼ teaspoon salt

1 cup sugar

½ cup (1 stick) unsalted butter, room temperature

2 teaspoons vanilla extract

5 eggs, room temperature

1 (5 ounce) can evaporated milk

1 (5 ounce) can sweetened condensed milk

½ cup heavy cream

¼ cup rum

FOR THE WHIPPED CREAM TOPPING

2 cups heavy whipping cream

¼ cup sugar

½ teaspoon vanilla extract

NUTRITION PER SERVING

Calories: 490

Fat: 31g

Sat Fat: 18g

Cholesterol: 190mg

Sodium: 240mg

Carbs: 47g

Fiber: 0g

Sugars: 31g

Protein: 7g

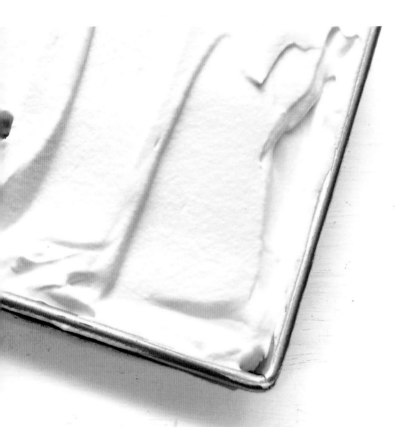

1 Preheat oven to 350°F. Lightly grease an 8 x 8-inch square cake pan with nonstick cooking spray and set aside.

2 To make the cake batter, in a medium bowl, whisk together brown rice flour, white rice flour, potato starch, baking powder, xanthan gum and salt.

3 In the bowl of a stand mixer using the paddle attachment, cream together sugar and butter until very light and fluffy, about 3 to 5 minutes.

4 Add vanilla extract and eggs, 1 at a time, beating well between each addition.

5 Slowly add dry ingredients into the wet ingredients, mixing well after each addition.

6 Pour batter into prepared cake pan and bake for 30 to 35 minutes or until a toothpick inserted into the center of the cake comes out with a few moist crumbs. Let cool in pan for 30 minutes.

7 In a small bowl, combine evaporated milk, condensed milk, heavy cream and rum. Whisk together well.

8 Once cake has cooled, gently prick the cake all over with a fork. Carefully pour milk mixture over the cake. Refrigerate and let soak for at least 4 hours or overnight.

9 To make the whipped cream topping, in the bowl of a stand mixer using the whisk attachment, beat together heavy whipping cream, sugar and vanilla extract until stiff peaks form. Refrigerate and frost cake with the whipped cream topping before serving.

PREP TIME
30 minutes

TOTAL TIME
1 hour

Black Forest Cake

The traditional flavors of chocolate and cherry come together in a delicious layer cake that is perfect for any occasion.

FOR THE CAKE BATTER

Nonstick cooking spray, for greasing cake pans

2 cups gluten-free all-purpose flour

1 ½ cups granulated sugar

¾ cup cocoa powder

½ cup brown sugar

2 teaspoons baking powder

1 teaspoon salt

2 eggs

1 ½ cups chocolate milk

½ cup vegetable oil

2 teaspoons vanilla extract

½ cup boiling water

FOR THE WHIPPED CREAM FILLING

1 cup heavy whipping cream

½ cup powdered sugar

1 tablespoon kirsch liqueur

2 cups cherries, pits removed, halved and divided

FOR THE GANACHE

8 ounces dark chocolate chips

½ cup heavy cream

2 teaspoons kirsch liqueur

Pinch of salt

NUTRITION PER SERVING

Calories: 560

Fat: 29g

Sat Fat: 13g

Cholesterol: 80mg

Sodium: 500mg

Carbs: 77g

Fiber: 6g

Sugars: 54g

Protein: 8g

1 Preheat oven to 350°F. Lightly grease 2 round 8-inch cake pans with nonstick cooking spray and set aside.

2 To make the cake batter, in a mixing bowl, whisk together gluten-free all-purpose flour, granulated sugar, cocoa powder, brown sugar, baking powder and salt.

3 In the bowl of a stand mixer using the paddle attachment, beat together eggs, chocolate milk, vegetable oil and vanilla extract.

4 Slowly add dry ingredients into the wet ingredients, mixing well after each addition. Slowly add boiling water and mix well until a smooth batter forms.

5 Divide batter evenly between 2 prepared cake pans and bake for 30 to 35 minutes until a toothpick inserted into the center of the cake comes out clean. Let cool completely on a cooling rack.

6 To make the whipped cream filling, in a stand mixer using the whisk attachment, whip cream until soft peaks form. Add powdered sugar and kirsch and beat until stiff peaks form.

7 To assemble the cake, place 1 cake on a cake stand or serving platter. Add ⅔ cup cherries in a single layer followed by whipped cream filling. Place other cake layer on top.

8 To make the ganache, in a double boiler combine chocolate chips, heavy cream, kirsch and salt and whisk together until chocolate is fully melted. Let cool to room temperature.

9 Pour ganache over assembled cake and top with remaining 1 ⅓ cups of cherries.

S'mores Cupcakes

These cupcakes make the perfect addition to a summer party or a camping trip! The traditional flavors of classic s'mores are reinvented into a cupcake that will bring back fond campfire memories.

FOR THE GRAHAM CRACKER CRUST

Paper liners, for lining muffin tins

1 ½ cups gluten-free graham cracker crumbs (like Kinnikinnick)

4 tablespoons (½ stick) butter, melted

1 tablespoon sugar

FOR THE CHOCOLATE CUPCAKE BATTER

2 cups gluten-free all-purpose flour

1 ½ cups granulated sugar

¾ cup cocoa powder

½ cup brown sugar

2 teaspoons baking powder

1 teaspoon salt

2 eggs

1 ½ cups coconut milk

½ cup vegetable oil

2 teaspoons vanilla extract

½ cup boiling water

FOR THE MARSHMALLOW FROSTING

6 egg whites

½ teaspoon cream of tartar

½ cup powdered sugar

1 teaspoon vanilla extract

1 Preheat oven to 350°F. Line 2 muffin tins with paper liners and set aside.

2 To make the graham cracker crust, in a mixing bowl, combine gluten-free graham cracker crumbs, melted butter and sugar. Mix together well. Gently press approximately 1 tablespoon of crumbs into the bottom of each of the liners and bake for 5 to 8 minutes until golden brown.

3 To make the chocolate cupcake batter, in a mixing bowl, whisk together gluten-free all-purpose flour, granulated sugar, cocoa powder, brown sugar, baking powder and salt.

4 In the bowl of a stand mixer using the paddle attachment, beat together eggs, coconut milk, vegetable oil and vanilla extract.

5 Slowly add dry ingredients into the wet ingredients, mixing well after each addition. Slowly add boiling water and mix well until a smooth batter forms.

6 Pour batter over crusts in the liners, filling about ¾ of the way full. Bake for 18 to 20 minutes until a toothpick inserted into the center of each cupcake comes out clean. Cool on a cooling rack.

7 To make the marshmallow frosting, in the bowl of a stand mixer using the whisk attachment, beat together egg whites and cream of tartar until soft peaks form. Add powdered sugar and vanilla extract and continue whisking until stiff peaks form and the mixture is glossy.

8 Frost cooled cupcakes with marshmallow frosting. Lightly brûlée tops with a kitchen torch, being careful not to burn the paper liners. If you don't have a torch, place cupcakes under the oven broiler on high for 2 to 3 minutes, watching closely to prevent burning.

YIELD
24 cupcakes

PREP TIME
30 minutes

TOTAL TIME
1 hour

NUTRITION PER SERVING
(1 cupcake)

Calories: 340

Fat: 15g

Sat Fat: 6g

Cholesterol: 30mg

Sodium: 320mg

Carbs: 50g

Fiber: 3g

Sugars: 32g

Protein: 5g

Banana Split Cupcakes

These cupcakes are perfect for a birthday party thanks to their traditional flavors and fun decorations. (See photo on pages 182–183.)

FOR THE CUPCAKE BATTER

Paper liners, for lining cupcake pans

2 cups gluten-free all-purpose flour

1 tablespoon baking powder

½ teaspoon salt

8 tablespoons (1 stick) butter, room temperature

2 cups sugar

4 eggs

¾ cup milk

¼ cup crushed peanuts, for garnish

1 (10 ounce) jar Maraschino cherries, for garnish

Sprinkles, for garnish

FOR THE BANANA CREAM FILLING

½ cup heavy whipping cream

¼ cup powdered sugar

1 ripe banana, mashed

1 teaspoon vanilla extract

FOR THE GANACHE

8 ounces bittersweet chocolate or chocolate chips, chopped

1 cup heavy cream

Pinch of salt

1 Preheat oven to 350°F. Line 2 cupcake pans with paper liners and set aside.

2 To make the cupcake batter, in a large bowl, whisk together gluten-free all-purpose flour, baking powder and salt. In a stand mixer using the paddle attachment, cream together butter and sugar until light and fluffy. Add eggs, 1 at a time, beating well after each addition.

3 Add milk slowly while beating on low speed. Add dry ingredients in 3 additions, mixing well between each one.

4 Divide batter evenly among prepared cupcake pans, filling each hole approximately ⅔ of the way full. Bake for 20 to 25 minutes until a toothpick inserted into the center of each cupcake comes out clean. Let cool for 5 minutes in the pans, then transfer to a cooling rack.

5 To make the banana cream filling, in the bowl of a stand mixer using the whisk attachment, whip heavy cream until soft peaks form. Add powdered sugar and banana and whip again until stiff peaks form. Add vanilla extract and blend in, being sure not to overwhip.

6 Cut out a small portion in the middle of the cooled cupcakes using a small knife or a very small biscuit cutter. Fill with banana cream. Place cupcakes in the refrigerator for 30 minutes.

7 To make the ganache, in a double boiler combine chocolate, heavy cream and salt and whisk together until chocolate is fully melted. Let cool for 15 minutes.

8 Set cupcakes on a rack set on top of parchment paper. Gently pour ganache over chilled cupcakes, then garnish with crushed peanuts, cherries and sprinkles. Place cupcakes in refrigerator for 5 minutes to allow ganache to harden.

NUTRITION PER SERVING
(1 cupcake)

Calories: 410

Fat: 23g

Sat Fat: 14g

Cholesterol: 110mg

Sodium: 280mg

Carbs: 52g

Fiber: 3g

Sugars: 37g

Protein: 5g

YIELD
8 servings

PREP TIME
10 minutes

TOTAL TIME
15 minutes

Pineapple Fools

These fools make the perfect quick dessert for unexpected guests or when you just want a little something cool and sweet.

6 cups finely diced fresh pineapple

1 cup plus 2 tablespoons sugar, divided

1 quart chilled heavy whipping cream

1 teaspoon vanilla extract

1 In a medium-sized saucepan, add pineapple and 1 cup sugar. Bring to a boil over medium-high heat, mashing pineapple until it is very soft and syrupy and most of the liquid has evaporated, about 20 minutes. Remove from heat and set aside to cool.

2 In the bowl of a stand mixer using the whisk attachment, whip heavy cream, remaining 2 tablespoons of sugar and vanilla extract until stiff peaks form.

3 To assemble the dessert, place a layer of whipped cream then a layer of pineapple in a clear glass. Alternate layers until the glass is full, ending with whipped cream.

NUTRITION PER SERVING

Calories: 480

Fat: 44g

Sat Fat: 28g

Cholesterol: 165mg

Sodium: 45mg

Carbs: 19g

Fiber: 0g

Sugars: 16g

Protein: 3g

Salted Chocolate Chip Cookies

YIELD
3 dozen cookies

PREP TIME
15 minutes

TOTAL TIME
35 minutes

These cookies have just a hint of salt to enhance the taste of the chocolate morsels and provide the slightest hint of salty-sweet flavor. Serve these cookies with a tall glass of milk!

Parchment paper, for lining cookie sheets

1 cup sweet white sorghum flour

1 cup tapioca flour

⅓ cup coconut flour

2 ½ teaspoons baking powder

1 ½ teaspoons salt

1 teaspoon xanthan gum

1 cup (2 sticks) butter, softened

¾ cup brown sugar

¾ cup granulated sugar

2 eggs, room temperature

2 tablespoons milk

2 teaspoons vanilla extract

1 cup chocolate chips

Sea salt, for garnish

1 Preheat oven to 350°F. Line 2 cookie sheets with parchment paper and set aside.

2 In a large mixing bowl, whisk together sorghum flour, tapioca flour, coconut flour, baking powder, salt and xanthan gum.

3 In the bowl of a stand mixer using the paddle attachment, cream together butter, brown sugar and granulated sugar until light and fluffy.

4 Add eggs, 1 at a time, into creamed sugars and mix well between each addition. Add milk and vanilla extract and mix well.

5 Slowly add dry ingredients into the wet ingredients, mixing well after each addition. Mix until a smooth dough forms. Gently fold in chocolate chips.

6 Drop dough by tablespoonful and place at least 2 inches apart on prepared cookie sheets. Using a fork, gently press the dough down flat.

7 Bake for 12 to 14 minutes until edges are lightly golden brown.

8 Remove cookies from oven and let cool on the cookie sheets for 2 to 3 minutes.

9 Sprinkle each cookie lightly with sea salt. Transfer to a cooling rack to cool completely.

NUTRITION PER SERVING
(1 cookie)

Calories: 130

Fat: 7g

Sat Fat: 4.5g

Cholesterol: 25mg

Sodium: 570mg

Carbs: 18g

Fiber: 1g

Sugars: 11g

Protein: 1g

Lemon Meringue Pie

A tart and tangy lemon curd fills this naturally gluten-free pie shell. If you're not in the mood for a pie, roll out the crust and use cookie cutters to cut out fun shapes. Top the cookies with a dollop of lemon curd and meringue topping for a twist on a traditional pie.

FOR THE PIE CRUST

1 cup brown rice flour

⅓ cup almond flour

½ cup sugar

1 teaspoon baking powder

5 tablespoons butter, room temperature

4 egg yolks

Zest of 2 lemons

1 teaspoon salt

Nonstick cooking spray, for greasing pie pan

FOR THE LEMON CURD

6 fluid ounces lemon juice, strained

Zest of 4 lemons

¾ cup sugar

½ cup unsalted butter

8 egg yolks (reserve 4 egg whites for meringue topping)

FOR THE MERINGUE TOPPING

4 egg whites

½ teaspoon cream of tartar

¼ cup sugar

½ teaspoon vanilla extract

1 To make the pie crust, in the bowl of a stand mixer using the paddle attachment, combine brown rice flour, almond flour, sugar and baking powder. Beat until well combined. Add butter, egg yolks, lemon zest and salt and mix until a smooth dough forms. Refrigerate dough for at least 30 minutes before using.

2 Preheat oven to 350°F. Grease a 9-inch pie pan with nonstick cooking spray. Roll dough out to approximately 10 inches and carefully press dough into prepared pie pan.

3 Bake for 12 to 15 minutes until golden brown. Cool completely before arranging filling on top.

4 To make the lemon curd, in a medium-sized saucepan, combine lemon juice, lemon zest, sugar and butter and bring to a boil over medium heat, whisking frequently.

5 In a separate bowl, whisk together egg yolks.

6 Beat approximately ¼ cup of boiling liquid into egg yolks to temper them and then whisk tempered mixture into the remaining lemon juice mixture over low heat, whisking vigorously. Continue whisking until the mixture thickens slightly, about 2 minutes. Do not let mixture boil.

7 Pour lemon curd over cooled pie crust and let cool completely.

8 To make the meringue topping, in the bowl of a stand mixer using the whisk attachment, whip egg whites and cream of tartar until soft peaks form. Gradually add sugar and vanilla extract and continue whisking until stiff peaks form. Scoop meringue on top of the lemon curd.

9 Preheat oven to 350°F. Bake for 5 to 7 minutes until the meringue is lightly browned. Cool completely and chill before serving.

NUTRITION PER SERVING

Calories: 410

Fat: 23g

Sat Fat: 12g

Cholesterol: 260mg

Sodium: 380mg

Carbs: 46g

Fiber: 1g

Sugars: 31g

Protein: 7g

Cherry Hand Pies

YIELD
16 individual pies

PREP TIME
30 minutes

TOTAL TIME
3 hours (includes chilling time)

Hand pies make perfect summer picnic desserts. These portable pies have a flaky crust and bright cherry filling that makes them a sure win with both kids and adults!

FOR THE PIE CRUST

2 cups brown rice flour

1 cup sugar

⅔ cup almond flour

2 teaspoons baking powder

10 tablespoons butter, room temperature

8 egg yolks

Zest of 2 lemons

2 teaspoons salt

Plastic wrap, for covering dough

Parchment paper, for lining baking sheet

FOR THE FILLING

3 cups frozen cherries

¼ cup sugar

1 tablespoon lemon zest

1 teaspoon vanilla extract

¼ cup fresh lemon juice

2 tablespoons cornstarch

FOR THE EGG WASH

1 egg

1 tablespoon water

1 To make the pie crust, in the bowl of a stand mixer using the paddle attachment, combine brown rice flour, sugar, almond flour and baking powder. Beat until well combined. Add butter, egg yolks, lemon zest and salt and mix until a smooth dough forms.

2 Roll dough into a ball and cover with plastic wrap. Refrigerate dough for at least 30 minutes before using.

3 To make the filling, in a saucepan, combine cherries, sugar, lemon zest and vanilla extract. Bring mixture to a boil over medium-high heat, mashing the cherries well. Boil mixture, stirring constantly, for 4 to 5 minutes.

4 In a small bowl, whisk together lemon juice and cornstarch. Add mixture to cherry mixture and stir vigorously until the filling has thickened, about 1 to 2 minutes. Remove from heat and let filling cool completely.

5 Remove dough from refrigerator and cut in half. Roll 1 piece of dough out to approximately a ½-inch-thick rectangle. Cut out 16 (4-inch) circles using the gluten-free floured rim of a water glass or a large biscuit cutter.

6 Roll out second piece of dough to approximately a ½-inch-thick rectangle. Cut out 16 (3-inch) circles using a slightly smaller biscuit cutter. Place each circle on a baking sheet lined with parchment paper.

7 Place approximately 1 tablespoon of filling in the center of each 3-inch dough circle. Gently lift 4-inch circles and place them on top of filling. Pinch edges together using wet fingers. Repeat until you have made all 16 hand pies. Chill pies for at least 30 minutes before baking.

8 Preheat oven to 375°F.

NUTRITION PER SERVING
(1 hand pie)

Calories: 300

Fat: 13g

Sat Fat: 6g

Cholesterol: 125mg

Sodium: 440mg

Carbs: 45g

Fiber: 2g

Sugars: 26g

Protein: 5g

9 To make the egg wash, in a small bowl, whisk together egg and water. Using a pastry brush, gently brush egg wash over pies. Slice a small slit in the top of each pie for venting.

10 Bake for 12 to 15 minutes or until golden brown. Cool slightly before serving.

Key Lime Crème Brûlée

Traditional crème brûlée gets a bright and light makeover thanks to the addition of a graham cracker crust and lime zest.

YIELD
6 servings

PREP TIME
30 minutes

TOTAL TIME
5 hours
(includes chilling time)

1 cup crushed gluten-free graham crackers

2 tablespoons butter, melted

1 quart heavy cream

2 teaspoons vanilla extract

¾ cup sugar, divided

2 teaspoons key lime or lime zest

6 egg yolks

2 ½ tablespoons key lime or lime juice

1 Preheat oven to 325°F. Prepare a large roasting pan with 6 4-inch ramekins and set aside.

2 In a bowl, combine graham crackers and melted butter and mix together well. Divide crust mixture evenly among ramekins and press firmly into each dish.

3 In a saucepan, add heavy cream and vanilla extract and heat over medium heat until just barely simmering. Let cool slightly.

4 In a small bowl, add ¼ cup sugar and key lime or lime zest and mix together with fingers until sugar is lightly colored and fragrant.

5 In a large bowl, whisk together remaining ½ cup of sugar, egg yolks and key lime or lime juice. Carefully add warm cream to egg yolk mixture, whisking constantly.

6 Pour mixture into ramekins. Pour hot water into roasting pan until it comes halfway up the sides of the ramekins.

7 Bake until crème brûlée is just barely set, about 45 to 50 minutes. Remove ramekins from water bath and refrigerate for at least 2 hours.

8 Top crème brûlées with prepared sugar and lime zest mixture and, using a kitchen torch, lightly melt sugar to form a crispy sugar top. If you don't have a torch, place under an oven broiler on high setting on the top rack for a few minutes, watching carefully to prevent burning.

NUTRITION PER SERVING

Calories: 840

Fat: 69g

Sat Fat: 41g

Cholesterol: 415mg

Sodium: 170mg

Carbs: 50g

Fiber: 0g

Sugars: 38g

Protein: 7g

YIELD
12 ice cream
sandwiches

PREP TIME
30 minutes

TOTAL TIME
8 hours
(includes
chilling time)

Brownie Ice Cream Sandwiches with Salted Caramel Ice Cream

These delightful ice cream sandwiches make a delicious treat for kids and adults alike. The combination of chocolate and salted caramel is rich, cool and satisfying. If you don't have the time or the energy to make homemade ice cream, simply substitute your favorite store-bought brand.

FOR THE ICE CREAM

1 ½ cups sugar

4 tablespoons (½ stick) butter

1 teaspoon sea salt

1 cup heavy cream

2 cups chilled whole milk, divided

5 egg yolks

1 teaspoon vanilla extract

FOR THE BROWNIES

Parchment paper or silicon mat, for lining baking sheet

1 cup gluten-free all-purpose flour

¼ cup cocoa powder

1 ½ teaspoons baking powder

1 teaspoon salt

6 tablespoons butter

1 cup chocolate chips

½ cup sugar

4 eggs

1 To make the ice cream, in a small skillet, add sugar in an even layer and heat over medium heat. Gently stir sugar constantly and cook until sugar has turned a deep golden caramel color.

2 Remove skillet from heat and add butter and sea salt. Gently whisk butter into sugar mixture. Once butter is melted, slowly whisk in heavy cream. The caramel may harden but continue cooking over low heat until melted once again. Stir in 1 cup milk and whisk until well combined.

3 In a separate bowl, whisk together egg yolks. Add a few spoonfuls of hot caramel mixture to egg yolks, whisking constantly. Add yolks into full caramel mixture and cook until thickened, stirring frequently and being sure to scrape the bottom as it cooks.

4 In a large bowl, add remaining 1 cup of milk and vanilla extract. Pour custard into milk and vanilla mixture and stir until fully combined. Continue to stir frequently to cool down the mixture. Refrigerate mixture for at least 8 hours or overnight until fully chilled. Churn in an ice cream maker according to manufacturer's instructions.

5 Preheat oven to 350°F. Line a baking sheet with parchment paper or a silicon mat and set aside.

6 To make the brownies, in the bowl of a stand mixer using the paddle attachment, beat together gluten-free all-purpose flour, cocoa powder, baking powder and salt.

7 In a small saucepan over medium heat, mix together butter, chocolate chips and sugar until melted. Add melted chocolate mixture to the flour mixture and beat until combined. Add eggs to the batter and beat until very well combined.

8 Pour batter onto prepared baking sheet and spread evenly across the surface. The batter should reach about 2 inches from each side of the baking sheet. Bake for 20 to 25 minutes until a toothpick inserted into the center of the brownies comes out clean. Let cool completely.

9 To assemble the ice cream sandwiches, cut brownie layer in half. Place 2 layers of brownies in freezer for 30 minutes.

10 Remove ice cream from the freezer and let it soften slightly. Spread ice cream over 1 brownie layer. Top with the other brownie layer and place it back in the freezer for 1 hour. Remove from freezer and cut into 12 ice cream sandwiches, using a biscuit cutter or a sharp knife. Keep frozen until ready to serve.

NUTRITION PER SERVING
(1 sandwich)

Calories: 460

Fat: 26g

Sat Fat: 15g

Cholesterol: 205mg

Sodium: 530mg

Carbs: 54g

Fiber: 3g

Sugars: 44g

Protein: 7g

YIELD
8 servings

PREP TIME
20 minutes

TOTAL TIME
1 hour
20 minutes

Flan de Coco

This flan recipe is made with a blend of sweetened condensed milk, evaporated milk, shredded coconut and other delightful flavors. Whipped cream adds a finishing touch to this tasty flan! Looking to cut down on calories? Try a reduced-fat condensed milk and light whipped cream!

Nonstick cooking spray, for greasing pie dish

1 cup granulated sugar

1 tablespoon plus ¼ teaspoon vanilla extract, divided

1 (12 ounce) can evaporated milk

1 (14 ounce) can sweetened condensed milk

6 whole eggs

¼ teaspoon salt

½ cup shredded unsweetened coconut flakes, plus additional for garnish

Whipped cream, for garnish

1 Preheat oven to 350°F. Spray a 9-inch glass pie dish with nonstick cooking spray and set aside.

2 In a small saucepan, stir together sugar and ¼ teaspoon vanilla extract over medium heat. Stir constantly until mixture is caramelized, about 10 to 12 minutes. Pour into prepared pie dish, coating the bottom.

3 In a blender, combine evaporated milk, condensed milk, eggs, 1 tablespoon vanilla extract, salt and coconut flakes. Pulse until a smooth mixture forms. Pour purée into prepared pie dish.

4 Prepare a water bath by placing the filled pie dish in a larger pan and adding enough water to reach halfway up the side of the pie dish.

5 Bake for 50 to 60 minutes or until a toothpick inserted into the center of the flan comes out clean. Let cool and serve topped with whipped cream and shredded coconut.

NUTRITION PER SERVING

Calories: 480

Fat: 15g

Sat Fat: 9g

Cholesterol: 200mg

Sodium: 250mg

Carbs: 71g

Fiber: 0g

Sugars: 69g

Protein: 13g

✪ Lemon Coconut Cake with Ginger Icing

YIELD
8 servings

PREP
10 minutes

TOTAL TIME
45 minutes

A soft and moist lemon pound cake is glazed with a citrus ginger frosting and topped with toasted coconut.

FOR THE CAKE BATTER

Nonstick cooking spray, for greasing bundt pan or cake pans

¾ cup skim milk

⅓ cup plus 2 teaspoons fresh lemon juice

2 tablespoons lemon zest

2 cups sugar

1 cup butter, softened

1 teaspoon vanilla extract

5 eggs

3 cups gluten-free all-purpose flour plus additional for dusting pans

1 ½ teaspoons salt

1 teaspoon baking powder

1 cup coconut flakes

FOR THE GINGER ICING

1 ½ cups confectioners powdered sugar

2 tablespoons milk

2 teaspoons fresh lemon juice

¼ teaspoon ground ginger

1 Preheat oven to 350°F. Grease a 12-cup bundt pan or 2 round cake pans with nonstick cooking spray and lightly dust with gluten-free all-purpose flour and set aside.

2 To make the cake batter, in a glass measuring cup, mix together skim milk, lemon juice and lemon zest. Stir well and set aside for 5 minutes.

3 In the bowl of a stand mixer using the paddle attachment, cream together sugar and butter. Mix until light and fluffy. Add vanilla extract and eggs, 1 at a time, mixing well after each addition.

4 In a separate bowl, whisk together gluten-free all-purpose flour, salt and baking powder.

5 With the stand mixer on low, add gluten-free flour mixture in 2 additions, alternating with lemon and milk mixture. Mix just until smooth.

6 Pour batter into prepared pan(s) and bake for 45 to 60 minutes (depending on pans) until a toothpick inserted into the center of the cake comes out clean. Cool for 15 minutes in pan(s) and then turn out onto a cooling rack. Cool completely before icing.

7 Spread coconut flakes onto a baking sheet. Bake at 325°F for 5 to 7 minutes, just until toasted. Watch coconut closely to prevent burning.

8 To make the ginger icing, mix powdered sugar, milk, lemon juice and ginger until smooth. Adjust consistency of the icing by adding more milk, as desired.

9 Drizzle ginger icing generously over lemon cake and top with toasted coconut. If using 2 cake pans, add a layer of icing in between the 2 cakes.

NUTRITION PER SERVING

Calories: 780

Fat: 34g

Sat Fat: 21g

Cholesterol: 195mg

Sodium: 800mg

Carbs: 115g

Fiber: 6g

Sugars: 81g

Protein: 11g

YIELD
8 servings

PREP TIME
10 minutes

TOTAL TIME
3 hours
10 minutes

Mangolicious Frozen Yogurt

A deliciously tropical recipe that blends together the flavors of fresh mangoes, bananas and yogurt, with just a hint of vanilla. For a variation in flavor, add a handful of fresh strawberries.

2 ripe mangoes, sliced

2 ripe bananas

2 cups plain yogurt

1 cup milk

1 cup granulated sugar

½ cup shredded unsweetened coconut flakes

1 tablespoon vanilla extract

1 In a blender, add mangoes, bananas, yogurt and milk and process until smooth.

2 Add sugar, coconut flakes and vanilla extract and blend until completely smooth.

3 Pour yogurt mixture into a freezer container and freeze for approximately 3 hours or until firm. If you have an ice cream maker, freeze yogurt according to manufacturer's instructions.

NUTRITION PER SERVING

Calories: 290

Fat: 8g

Sat Fat: 6g

Cholesterol: 10mg

Sodium: 35mg

Carbs: 49g

Fiber: 3g

Sugars: 44g

Protein: 6g

Chocolate-Dipped Marzipan Pops

A scrumptious confection made with naturally gluten-free almond meal. The pops are dipped to perfection in semisweet chocolate and topped with sprinkles. Not a fan of sprinkles? Try dipping the pops in crushed nuts or shredded coconut.

Parchment paper, for lining baking sheets

4 cups almond meal

2 egg whites

1 teaspoon vanilla extract

2 cups granulated sugar

⅔ cup water

¼ teaspoon cream of tartar

¾ cup powdered sugar

20 lollipop sticks

½ cup water

1 (24 ounce) package semisweet chocolate morsels

Colored sprinkles, for garnish

1 Line 2 baking sheets with parchment paper and set aside.

2 In a large bowl, whisk together almond meal, egg whites and vanilla extract.

3 In a saucepan, dissolve sugar in water over medium-high heat, whisking constantly. Bring mixture to a boil, whisk in cream of tartar and cover and simmer for 3 minutes. Remove mixture from heat.

4 Gradually whisk in almond meal mixture to sugar mixture. Continue to stir until well combined.

5 Dust 1 of the parchment-lined baking sheets with powdered sugar. Pour marzipan mixture over powdered sugar and let cool until slightly firm, about 5 minutes.

6 Dust your hands with powdered sugar and shape marzipan into 1-inch balls. Place balls on the second parchment-lined baking sheet. Freeze balls for approximately 15 minutes.

7 Remove from freezer and stack 2 marzipan balls per lollipop stick.

8 Bring water to a boil and stir in chocolate morsels. Continue to stir until chocolate has melted. Dip each marzipan pop into melted chocolate and then roll pops into sprinkles or other desired toppings.

9 Place marzipan pops on parchment paper to prevent them from sticking. Let cool and allow chocolate to harden.

YIELD
20 servings

PREP TIME
20 minutes

TOTAL TIME
1 hour
30 minutes

NUTRITION PER SERVING

Calories: 410

Fat: 23g

Sat Fat: 7g

Cholesterol: 0mg

Sodium: 10mg

Carbs: 51g

Fiber: 4g

Sugars: 45g

Protein: 7g

YIELD
40 cookies

PREP TIME
10 minutes

TOTAL TIME
50 minutes

Macadamia Meringues

Crunchy macadamia nuts add a new twist to this traditional recipe, making these meringues the ideal treat for any special occasion. Delightfully flavored with a hint of vanilla extract.

Parchment paper, for lining baking sheets

1 cup granulated sugar

½ teaspoon cream of tartar

¼ teaspoon salt

4 egg whites, room temperature

½ teaspoon vanilla extract

40 macadamia nuts

Colored sprinkles, for garnish (optional)

1 Preheat oven to 300°F. Line 2 baking sheets with parchment paper and set aside.

2 In a mixing bowl, stir together sugar, cream of tartar and salt.

3 In the bowl of a stand mixer using the whisk attachment, add egg whites and mix at high speed until soft peaks form.

4 Continue to mix while adding vanilla extract. Gradually add sugar mixture and continue whisking on high speed until meringue mixture is stiff and glossy.

5 Place macadamia nuts about 1 inch apart on prepared baking sheets. Drop meringue mixture by tablespoonful on top of each macadamia nut and top with sprinkles, if desired.

6 Bake for 40 minutes or until set but not brown. Let cool before serving.

NUTRITION PER SERVING
(1 cookie)

Calories: 40

Fat: 2g

Sat Fat: 0g

Cholesterol: 0mg

Sodium: 20mg

Carbs: 6g

Fiber: 0g

Sugars: 5g

Protein: 1g

Guava Shortbread Cookies

Scrumptious shortbread cookies that are topped with guava jelly for a flavorful kick!

Parchment paper, for lining baking sheets

1 cup granulated sugar

½ cup (1 stick) salted butter

½ cup vegetable shortening

2 egg yolks

2 tablespoons water

2 teaspoons almond extract

2 teaspoons vanilla extract

2 ½ cups all-purpose gluten-free flour

½ cup guava jelly

Colored sprinkles, for garnish (optional)

1 Preheat oven to 350°F. Line 2 baking sheets with parchment paper and set aside.

2 In the bowl of a stand mixer using the paddle attachment, beat together sugar, butter, vegetable shortening, egg yolks, water, almond extract and vanilla extract until light and creamy.

3 Slowly add gluten-free all-purpose flour and mix until a smooth dough forms.

4 Drop dough by tablespoonful onto prepared baking sheets about 1 inch apart and lightly press in the center of each cookie.

5 Fill center of each cookie with guava jelly and top with sprinkles if desired.

6 Bake for 12 to 15 minutes or until lightly golden. Let cool before serving.

**NUTRITION
PER SERVING**
(1 cookie)

Calories: 100

Fat: 5g

Sat Fat: 2g

Cholesterol: 15mg

Sodium: 20mg

Carbs: 13g

Fiber: 1g

Sugars: 8g

Protein: 1g

Nut Butter Sandwich Cookies

A tasty sandwich cookie filled to perfection with a homemade blend of lightly salted peanuts and cocoa powder. For a variation in flavor, substitute peanuts and peanut butter with your choice of nuts and nut butter. Shredded coconut makes the perfect garnish!

YIELD
16 cookie
sandwiches

PREP TIME
20 minutes

TOTAL TIME
35 minutes

FOR THE COOKIE FILLING

2 cups lightly salted peanuts

1 ¼ cups powdered sugar

⅓ cup cocoa powder

½ cup vegetable oil

2 teaspoons vanilla extract

FOR THE COOKIES

Parchment paper, for lining baking sheets

2 cups creamy peanut butter

1 cup granulated sugar

2 eggs

2 teaspoons baking powder

½ teaspoon salt

⅓ cup shredded unsweetened coconut, for garnish (optional)

1 To make the cookie filling, in a food processor, combine peanuts, powdered sugar, cocoa powder, vegetable oil and vanilla extract and pulse until smooth. Cover and place in the refrigerator for at least 30 minutes before using.

2 Preheat oven to 350°F. Line 2 baking sheets with parchment paper and set aside.

3 To make the cookies, in the bowl of a stand mixer using the paddle attachment, beat together peanut butter, sugar, eggs, baking powder and salt until a smooth dough forms.

4 Drop dough by tablespoonful onto prepared baking sheets, about 1 inch apart. With your fingers, gently press dough into flat disks.

5 Bake for 12 to 15 minutes or until lightly golden. Let cool completely.

6 To assemble the nut butter sandwich cookies, fill 2 cookies by spreading a teaspoon of the chocolate filling between them. Repeat until all cookies are sandwiched with filling. Roll edges of the cookie sandwiches in shredded coconut, if desired.

NUTRITION PER SERVING
(1 cookie)

Calories: 380

Fat: 27g

Sat Fat: 3.5g

Cholesterol: 20mg

Sodium: 220mg

Carbs: 27g

Fiber: 3g

Sugars: 20g

Protein: 10g

Cocktails

Raspberry Lime Sangria – page 244

Blackberry Wine Spritzers

If you're having a dinner party, make this as instructed below. If it's a night alone at home, just make smaller portions of the recipe in individual glasses rather than a large pitcher. Simply muddle the berries and lime juice in a glass and then top with sparkling wine and soda.

1 cup fresh blackberries

3 tablespoons lime juice

1 bottle sweet sparkling wine
(sparkling Riesling or Moscato)

1 cup lemon-lime soda

Ice

1 In a large pitcher, muddle together blackberries and lime juice.

2 Add sparkling wine and lemon-lime soda and stir well.

3 Serve immediately over ice.

Ginger Pineapple Banana Daiquiris

A pinch of ginger gives a mighty zing to this classic pineapple banana daiquiri! You'll feel like you're in the tropics as you enjoy this cocktail!

1 cup diced pineapple

2 bananas, roughly chopped

1 cup canned coconut milk

2 tablespoons lime juice

¼ cup agave nectar

4 fluid ounces white rum

½ teaspoon ground ginger

5 to 6 cups ice

Pineapple slices, for garnish

1 In a blender, combine all ingredients and purée until smooth.

2 Pour mixture into glasses and garnish with a pineapple slice.

Blueberry Basil Lemonade Coolers

Tart, sweet and fizzy all at the same time, this summertime cocktail is simple to make and big on taste! If mock-tails are more your style, just omit the vodka. It's a nice addition, but definitely not necessary to enjoy these spectacular flavors.

YIELD
16 servings

PREP TIME
30 minutes

TOTAL TIME
35 minutes

V

1 (12 ounce) jar frozen lemonade

1 cup water

1 cup fresh or frozen blueberries

12 large basil leaves

Ice

1 ½ fluid ounces (1 shot) vodka, per serving

Club soda or sparkling water, for serving

Additional basil leaves, for garnish (optional)

Additional blueberries, for garnish (optional)

1 In a medium-sized saucepan, mix together lemonade, water, blueberries and basil leaves. Cook, stirring frequently, over medium heat until mixture comes to a rolling boil.

2 Reduce heat to low and simmer for 15 minutes until mixture thickens and becomes syrupy.

3 Remove from heat and pour mixture through a fine mesh strainer to remove basil leaves and blueberry pulp. Cool completely.

4 To assemble the blueberry basil lemonade coolers, in each cocktail glass filled with ice, add 4 tablespoons of syrup. Add vodka and fill glass with club soda or sparkling water. Stir together well. Garnish with basil leaves and blueberries, if desired.

NUTRITION PER SERVING

Calories: 150

Fat: 0g

Sat Fat: 0g

Cholesterol: 0mg

Sodium: 10mg

Carbs: 14g

Fiber: 0g

Sugars: 13g

Protein: 0g

Cucumber Lime Gin & Ginger

Not your average gin and tonic! This light and fresh cocktail blends together the clean flavor of cucumber with tart lime juice. This cocktail is great for a warm evening on the balcony.

Ice
5 thin slices cucumber
2 lime wedges
1 ½ fluid ounces (1 shot) gin
1 (12 ounce) can ginger ale

1 To a cocktail glass filled with ice, add cucumber slices. Squeeze lime juice from wedges into glass and place squeezed wedges into glass.

2 Pour gin into glass and fill with ginger ale.

Skinny Guava Mojito

Tropical and fruity, this drink is sweetened with just a hint of agave nectar.

⅛ cup mint leaves
2 teaspoons agave nectar
3 thinly sliced lime wedges
Ice
½ cup guava juice
½ cup sparkling water
1 ½ fluid ounces (1 shot) white rum

1 In the bottom of a cocktail glass, muddle together mint leaves, agave nectar and lime wedges.

2 Add a large handful of ice to the glass and top with guava juice, sparkling water and white rum. Mix together well before serving.

Grapefruit Smash

Not your typical grapefruit cocktail! The bitter grapefruit flavor is sweetened with sugar and whiskey. Great for both gents and ladies!

YIELD
1 cocktail

PREP TIME
5 minutes

TOTAL TIME
5 minutes

V

3 grapefruit segments

1 teaspoon sugar

Ice

1 ounce whiskey

Ginger ale

Small grapefruit segment or peel, for garnish

1 Add grapefruit segments and sugar to a glass. Muddle together until grapefruit has released its juices.

2 Add ice and whiskey to the glass and gently stir to combine. Top with ginger ale and serve garnished with grapefruit segment or peel.

NUTRITION PER SERVING

Calories: 470

Fat: 0.5g

Sat Fat: 0g

Cholesterol: 0mg

Sodium: 45mg

Carbs: 109g

Fiber: 7g

Sugars: 37g

Protein: 4g

FAN FAVORITE

YIELD
1 cocktail

PREP TIME
5 minutes

TOTAL TIME
10 minutes

**NUTRITION
PER SERVING**

Calories: 200

Fat: 0g

Sat Fat: 0g

Cholesterol:
0mg

Sodium: 0mg

Carbs: 19g

Fiber: 1g

Sugars: 12g

Protein: 1g

Watermelon Aqua Fresca

Fresh watermelon is the base of this light and fresh cocktail. If you'd prefer a different melon, simply substitute honeydew or cantaloupe for an equally delightful beverage.

1 cup diced fresh watermelon
Ice
2 ounces vodka
¼ cup fresh lime juice
Fresh or frozen raspberries, for garnish (optional)

1 Blend fresh watermelon chunks, using a blender. Strain into a glass with ice, using a fine mesh strainer.

2 Add vodka and lime juice and gently stir to mix. Garnish with fresh or frozen raspberries, if desired.

★ Chocolate Hazelnut Martini

YIELD
1 cocktail

PREP TIME
5 minutes

TOTAL TIME
10 minutes

Sweet, rich and sinfully delicious, this cocktail will be the hit of your winter dinner party. Just be sure to buy plenty of ingredients because most guests will want more than one.

Melted chocolate or chocolate sauce
Ice
2 ounces chocolate liqueur
1 ounce vanilla vodka
½ ounce hazelnut liqueur

1 Gently rim glass with melted chocolate. Chill in the freezer.

2 In a shaker filled with ice, combine chocolate liqueur, vanilla vodka and hazelnut liqueur and shake vigorously. Strain and pour into prepared chilled glass.

NUTRITION PER SERVING

Calories: 330

Fat: 0g

Sat Fat: 0g

Cholesterol: 0mg

Sodium: 30mg

Carbs: 25g

Fiber: 1g

Sugars: 19g

Protein: 1g

YIELD
1 large pitcher
(8 servings)

PREP TIME
5 minutes

TOTAL TIME
10 minutes

Raspberry Lime Sangria

A twist on the classic sangria recipe, this recipe uses raspberries and limes in place of the usual oranges, apples and pears.

Ice

12 ounces fresh raspberries

4 limes, thinly sliced into rounds

1 bottle white zinfandel or rosé wine

2 cups limeade

½ cup orange liqueur, such as Grand Marnier

1 Fill a large pitcher with ice and add raspberries and lime slices.

2 Add wine, limeade and orange liqueur and stir well. Serve immediately.

NUTRITION PER SERVING

Calories: 150

Fat: 0g

Sat Fat: 0g

Cholesterol: 0mg

Sodium: 10mg

Carbs: 18g

Fiber: 1g

Sugars: 7g

Protein: 0g

YIELD
16 servings

PREP TIME
30 minutes

TOTAL TIME
35 minutes

Strawberry Mint Limeade Sparklers

This easy-to-make strawberry lime simple syrup can serve as the base for so many drinks! If you love sweeter drinks, replace the club soda with a lemon-lime–type soda.

1 (12 ounce) jar frozen limeade

1 cup water

2 cups sliced fresh or frozen strawberries

12 mint leaves

Ice

1 ½ fluid ounces (1 shot) vodka, per serving

Club soda or sparkling water, for serving

Additional strawberries, for garnish (optional)

1 In a medium-sized saucepan, mix together limeade, water, strawberries and mint leaves. Cook, stirring frequently, over medium heat until mixture comes to a rolling boil.

2 Reduce heat to low and simmer for 15 minutes until mixture thickens and becomes syrupy.

3 Remove from heat and pour mixture through a fine mesh strainer to remove mint leaves and strawberry pulp. Cool completely.

4 To assemble the strawberry mint limeade sparklers, in each cocktail glass filled with ice, add 4 tablespoons of syrup. Add vodka and fill glass with club soda or sparkling water. Stir together well. Garnish with strawberries, if desired.

NUTRITION PER SERVING

Calories: 110

Fat: 0g

Sat Fat: 0g

Cholesterol: 0mg

Sodium: 0mg

Carbs: 5g

Fiber: 0g

Sugars: 4g

Protein: 0g

Converting to Metrics

Volume Measurement Conversions

U.S.	Metric
¼ teaspoon	1.25 ml
½ teaspoon	2.5 ml
¾ teaspoon	3.75 ml
1 teaspoon	5 ml
1 tablespoon	15 ml
¼ cup	62.5 ml
½ cup	125 ml
¾ cup	187.5 ml
1 cup	250 ml

Weight Conversion Measurements

U.S.	Metric
1 ounce	28.4 g
8 ounces	227.5 g
16 ounces (1 pound)	455 g

Cooking Temperature Conversions

Celsius/Centigrade

0°C and 100°C are arbitrarily placed at the melting and boiling points of water and standard to the metric system.

Fahrenheit

Fahrenheit established 0°F as the stabilized temperature when equal amounts of ice, water and salt are mixed.

To convert temperatures in Fahrenheit to Celsius, use this formula:

C = (F – 32) x 0.5555

So, for example, if you are baking at 350°F and want to know that temperature in Celsius, use this calculation:

C = (350 – 32) x 0.5555 = 176.6°C

Index

About the Author

Vanessa Maltin Weisbrod is the executive editor of *Delight Gluten-Free Magazine* and the author of *The Gloriously Gluten-Free Cookbook* (Wiley, 2010). Weisbrod has been featured on Planet Green's *Emeril Green*, CNBC's *On the Money* and CNN's *Newsroom with Heidi Collins*, and also in *U.S. News & World Report*, *Newsweek* and the *Washington Post*, among many other publications. A graduate of the Institute of Culinary Education, she is an active member of the Advisory Board of the Celiac Program at Children's National Medical Center. She lives in Silver Spring, Maryland. To learn more, visit delightglutenfree.com.

★ Recipe Notes ★